From Enmity to Alliance

U.S.-AUSTRALIAN RELATIONS, 1931-1941

From Enmity to Alliance

U.S.-AUSTRALIAN RELATIONS, 1931-1941

RAYMOND A. ESTHUS

University of Washington Press   *Seattle*

First Edition
Copyright © 1964 by the University of Washington Press
Library of Congress Catalog Card Number 64-20486
Manufactured by George Banta Company, Inc., Menasha, Wisconsin
Printed in the United States of America

To My Parents:
Arthur Engen Esthus
Clara Andersen Esthus

Preface

ANGLO-AMERICAN relations have been the mainspring of American foreign policy since the time of independence. As Anglo-American enmity was the fountainhead of United States diplomacy in the nineteenth century, so Anglo-American friendship has been the pivot of United States policy in the twentieth century. Many studies have been made which treat the diplomacy between Washington and London, but little has thus far been done on the relations between the United States and the self-governing Dominions of the British Commonwealth, other than Canada where territorial contiguity has dictated a special interest. As the Dominions emerged as distinct international entities in the years following the First World War, their policies came to occupy a larger and larger place in the overall picture of United States-British Commonwealth relations. The opening of Department of State records now permits the study of this aspect of Anglo-American relations in the period between the two world wars.

This book recounts the relations between the United States and Australia in the ten years preceding the wartime alliance of World War II. This period saw Australia assume growing importance in Pacific affairs, culminating with the opening of formal diplomatic relations with Washington, Tokyo, and Chungking in 1940-1941. With the approach of the Pacific War the connection between Canberra and Washington became increasingly vital. The story of this decade is not an altogether happy one, for acrimonious disputes over shipping competition and trade created enmity and antagonism in the early and middle 1930's. Not until late in the decade did Australia's involvement in the European War and the threat of a Pacific War compel a reorientation in the relations between the United States and Australia. The Australian-American rapprochement thus came four decades later than the great turn-of-the-century Anglo-American rapprochement.

In relating United States-Australian relations I have had to range beyond the central story of diplomacy between Canberra

vii

and Washington. The role of the United Kingdom looms so large that the study is to some extent an analysis of triangular diplomacy among London, Canberra, and Washington. Also, as the narrative moves into the late 1930's, it recounts the coming of the Pacific war. The diplomacy preceding the war has already been chronicled in the excellent studies by Butow, Feis, and Langer and Gleason; and I have not attempted to redo their work. Though some revelations have subsequently been made from records of the United Kingdom and the Dominions—and are here incorporated—the basic story stands as they have given it. It is hoped, however, that by focusing upon the United States-Australian side of the U.S.-U.K.-Australian triangle, an additional perspective will be provided for the crucial diplomacy preceding Pearl Harbor.

The manuscript has been read at various stages of preparation by Alexander DeConde, Norman A. Graebner, and C. Hartley Grattan. I wish to express appreciation for their thoughtful and critical comments. I am indebted to Mrs. Albert Lévitt, widow of Jay Pierrepont Moffat, for granting access to the Moffat papers and for saving me from several errors by a careful reading of the manuscript. I wish to thank also Dr. E. Taylor Parks, who facilitated use of the Department of State records. My most longstanding indebtedness is to Dr. Paul C. Clyde, who some years ago nudged me, as an innocent fledgling, into the vicissitudes of American Far Eastern policy, and who later pointed out to me the need for studies in United States-Australian relations.

RAYMOND A. ESTHUS

Tulane University

Acknowledgments

Pᴇʀᴍɪssɪᴏɴ for the use of passages of copyrighted material from the following publishers and authors is gratefully acknowledged: Angus and Robertson, for *John Curtin,* by Alan Chester, and *Truant Surgeon,* by Sir Earle Page; Little, Brown, and Co., for *The Rising Sun in the Pacific (History of United States Naval Operations in World War II,* Vol. III), by Samuel Eliot Morison; Harper and Row, for *Roosevelt and Hopkins,* by Robert E. Sherwood, and *The Undeclared War,* by William L. Langer and S. Everett Gleason; Harvard University Press, for *The Moffat Papers,* edited by Nancy Harvison Hooker; Houghton Mifflin, for *The Grand Alliance* and *Their Finest Hour,* by Winston S. Churchill; Hutchinson and Company, for *Carpenter to Cabinet,* by Sir George Pearce; The Macmillan Company, for *The Memoirs of Cordell Hull;* Macmillan and Company, for *The Life of Neville Chamberlain,* by Keith Feiling, and *Lord Lothian,* by J. R. M. Butler; Princeton University Press, for *The Road to Pearl Harbor,* by Herbert Feis; The War Memorial (Australia), for *The Government and the People,* by Paul Hasluck, and *The Japanese Thrust,* by Lionel Wigmore.

Contents

From Enmity to Alliance

U.S.-AUSTRALIAN RELATIONS, 1931-1941

CHAPTER ONE

The United States and Australia
in the Era of the World Depression

IN THE dark days of December, 1941, when Japanese forces were driving across the Southwest Pacific, Prime Minister John Curtin published a message to the Australian people in which he asserted in unqualified terms that Australia looked to the United States, rather than to the United Kingdom, for its security:

> The Australian Government [he declared] regards the Pacific struggle as primarily one in which the United States and Australia must have the fullest say in the direction of the Democracies fighting plan. Without any inhibitions of any kind, I make it quite clear that Australia looks to America, free of any pangs as to our traditional links or kinship with the United Kingdom. We know the problems that the United Kingdom faces. We know the constant threat of invasion. We know the dangers of dispersal of strength. But we know too that Australia can go, and Britain can still hold on.
> We are therefore determined that Australia shall not go, and we shall exert all our energies toward shaping of a plan, with the United States as its keystone, which will give to our country some confidence of being able to hold out until the tide of battle swings against the enemy.[1]

So far as sentiment to the mother country was concerned, Curtin's remarks did not accurately mirror Australian feeling—as many of his countrymen were quick to remind him—but in terms of strategic considerations his statement was a correct appreciation of the new power relationship that had evolved. By December, 1941, the United States had become the most important factor in Australian security, a relationship which was to continue throughout the war and into the postwar era. Into the 1960's the strategic ties between

3

the United States and Australia have remained firm and they appear likely to remain so.

A decade before the outbreak of the Pacific war the position occupied by the United States in Australian external affairs and strategic considerations was of far less significance than that held by the United Kingdom. The cords binding Australia to the home country were many and strong. The connection transcended constitutional ties, for it was "a product in part of kinship with and sentiment for Britain, in part also of certain strategical and economic factors."[2] The strong sentiment of attachment was evident even among the more nationally minded members of Australian society. Typical of this feeling was a statement by a Labour member of the House of Representatives in June, 1940: "The workers of Australia do not look on England merely as a place where they can sell goods and borrow money. England is the home of our race; we love England, and if England should go down it would seem to me as if the sun went down."[3]

Strategic and economic considerations also linked Australia closely with the United Kingdom. Australia's navy, which in 1930 consisted of two cruisers in commission with two cruisers, five destroyers, and two submarines in reserve, was of little strategic significance except as a part of the mighty navy of the Commonwealth and Empire. In matters of trade—Australia's life blood—the United Kingdom dominated, taking almost half of Australia's exports and furnishing close to half her imports.[4] Australia also depended upon the London money market for development funds, borrowing about thirty million pounds a year until the world depression dried up capital sources.

Constitutional ties had long bound Australia closely to the home country. In the 1920's and 1930's however, that relationship underwent considerable change. The Balfour Declaration of 1926 had set forth the framework for Australia's evolving position in the British Commonwealth. That famous dictum declared that the autonomous communities within the British Empire were equal in status, in no way subordinate one to another in any aspect of their domestic and external affairs, though united by a common allegiance to the crown. The Statute of Westminster of 1931, which gave legal sanction to the Balfour Declaration, was not adopted by Australia until

1942, but throughout the 1930's an increasing sense of distinct nationhood pervaded Australia.

In the early 1930's the United States was second only to the United Kingdom in Australian strategic and economic considerations, but it ranked far behind the home country. The formal ties between the United States and Australia were weak and inadequate. The United States had consulates in Melbourne, Adelaide, and Newcastle, and a consulate general at Sydney. Australia had only a trade commissioner in the United States, and he was situated not at Washington but at New York and concerned himself exclusively with matters of trade. Diplomatic matters were handled by the British ambassador at Washington. Since the time of the Paris Peace Conference, Australia might have exchanged ministers with the United States, but though the United States would have welcomed such a development, Australia held back. Australian leaders always pleaded insufficient need and lack of funds, but there was doubtless an additional and perhaps more weighty reason: the preference for the diplomatic interposition of the United Kingdom. The big diplomatic guns of the British embassy seemed preferable to the uncertain status of an Australian legation at Washington.

The lack of an Australian diplomatic representative in the United States was unfortunate. The Australian government remained poorly informed about American affairs. The American consulate general at Sydney kept the United States government in close touch with governmental operations at Canberra, but the Australian leaders, having no comparable source of information, relied heavily upon press dispatches from Australian and British correspondents in the United States. The results were bad, for these reports gave the worst possible picture of the United States. In 1931 Consul General Roger C. Tredwell reported:

> The press in Sydney, and throughout Australia generally have followed their usual custom of emphasizing and giving prominence to every cable item of news from America which reflects upon the character of its Government and people. It is unfortunate that only the worst part of American life is cabled abroad by correspondents of the Australian press in the United States. This not only makes for a great deal of ill-will, but increases misunderstandings, and . . . leads a large number of people to the conclusion that Americans are the most wicked and the worst people in the world.[5]

The lack of formal diplomatic relations was not the only, nor indeed the greatest trouble besetting United States-Australian relations in the early 1930's. More serious was the presence of an enormous amount of ill-will which had been accumulating in the years since the First World War. It is difficult for those who have observed the close and friendly relations between the two countries during and after the Second World War to imagine the extent of this ill feeling. Yet at every hand the historical records attest to its existence. In 1935 the Australian Minister for External Affairs, Sir George Pearce, could state with much accuracy that Australian-American relations had reached their zenith during the visit of the "Great White Fleet" in 1908, and they had been going downhill ever since.[6]

In Australia the resentment against the United Sates was based upon a long list of grievances, many growing out of World War I. The first jarring shock to Australian friendship was America's long delay in entering the war. Then came the rejection of the Versailles treaty by the United States Senate and the resulting refusal to join the League of Nations. The subsequent insistence by the United States that the war debts be paid caused intense bitterness in Australia. When the world depression came in 1929, Australians were quick to hold American economic policies responsible for the disaster. Consul Albert M. Doyle reported to Secretary of State Henry L. Stimson in June, 1932:

> Discussion of the world economic depression, both in the press and in business and economic publications, continues to lay blame upon the policy of the United States of insisting upon payment of war debts. Discussion of the merits of the question have largely ceased and it is assumed, as a thesis not requiring further proof, in most of these articles that the United States is fundamentally wrong in its attitude.[7]

The world depression greatly accentuated the existing tensions between the two countries. This was especially true of the long-standing friction over trade. On the Australian side there was deep irritation over the high American tariffs which effectively kept out most of Australia's principal exports. The biggest complaint concerned the high duty on wool. The rate, already high before 1930, was raised in that year from thirty-one cents to thirty-four cents per pound. In the face of the disastrous price drops of the depression, the *ad valorem* equivalent of this rate rose to over eighty-nine per cent in 1931.[8] Australians were convinced that these high rates were responsible for the consistently unfavorable balance of trade with the United States, and British commercial interests in Australia were not slow to use the issue to their advantage. In 1931 the Australian Association of British Manufacturers issued a pamphlet entitled "One-Way Traffic—Australia's Trade with the United States." The publication urged Australians not to purchase goods made in the United States or to patronize American films, for by so doing they would be applying Australia's hard-earned foreign exchange in a direction from which no reciprocity could be expected. "The United States export policy," the pamphlet stated, "is to sell American goods in other countries and at the same time raise a tariff wall of almost insurmountable height to keep out certain goods produced by foreign competition—including Australia." With that thesis most Australians readily agreed.

In the United States a similar resentment simmered over high Australian tariffs, though it was more limited to governmental and business circles than was the case in Australia. The wide margin of preference given to the Empire aroused particular bitterness. As far back as 1908 Australia had introduced a dual column tariff giving preference to the United Kingdom, generally five per cent. By 1931 some preference margins had reached as much as twenty per cent. American complaints against the Australian tariff waxed even stronger with the inauguration of a more comprehensive program of imperial preference at the Ottawa conference in 1932. Under the Ottawa program Australia agreed to give minimum margins ranging from fifteen to twenty per cent.[9] The government of Joseph A. Lyons, which replaced the Labour government of James H. Scullin in 1932, began a program of tariff reduction, but as the rates were lowered the margin of preference was often increased. Of all the Dominions in the Commonwealth, Australia during the 1930's had the highest tariff rates and was also granting the widest margin of preference to the United Kingdom on the greatest number of items.[10]

The tariff issue led to recriminations on both sides, each feeling that the other imposed the higher rates. It would be difficult to assess which country's rates were the most unreasonable, but one fact was crystal clear: year after year Australia suffered a stagger-

ingly unfavorable balance of trade with the United States. In the
year ending June 30, 1928, American motor cars and parts, petroleum products, timber, tobacco, tractors, and other items com-
prised twenty-four per cent of Australia's total imports. The value
of these products amounted to $141,440,000. In return the United
States purchased only six per cent of Australia's exports. The value
of these products, largely wool, furs, and cattle hides, amounted to
only $31,577,000, leaving Australia with an unfavorable balance
of trade amounting to $109,863,000. During the depression years
the volume of trade declined sharply, but the ratio remained approximately the same with the United States selling four to six
times as much as it bought from Australia.[11]

The unfavorable balance of trade was the principal source of
Australia's resentment toward the United States, but the absence
of a trade treaty caused additional difficulties. Anglo-American
trade was conducted under the treaty of 1815, which by its terms
was limited to "all the Territories of His Britannic Majesty in Europe." Since no United States-Australian trade treaty had ever been
concluded, Australians had no treaty rights of entry and residence
in the United States. When the United States passed restrictive im-
migration legislation in 1924, Australian businessmen who wished
to enter the United States were henceforth compelled to enter
either under the quota system (one hundred and twenty-one per
year from Australia) or as temporary visitors. Visitors' permits
were usually renewed, but the inconvenience and uncertainty inherent in their status created considerable discontent among Australian businessmen. Though American businessmen in Australia
suffered from no such impediment, the United States rebuffed Australian requests for an *ad hoc* treaty on entry and residence. Spo-
radic negotiations on the issue were carried on through the British
embassy for more than eight years, but these were terminated in
1934 without result. In American governmental circles so much resentment existed over Australia's high tariffs and imperial preference margins that officials were not disposed to do anything bene-
fitting the Australians without a *quid pro quo* over and above the
entry and residence privileges which Americans were enjoying in
Australia. Under Secretary of State Joseph P. Cotton accurately expressed this feeling in 1930 when he noted in a State Department
memorandum that the status of Australian businessmen in the

United States was "not nearly as unsatisfactory as the present status of American businessmen in Australia, whose trade is subject to tariff discriminations of an almost ferocious sort."[12]

In 1931 another contentious issue, destined to plague United States-Australian relations for seven years, arose. In July of that year the Matson Navigation Company added Auckland, New Zealand, as a port of call. The American-owned Matson line had served the San Francisco-Sydney route for many years without causing controversy, but by adding Auckland the company now offered passenger service between New Zealand and Australia. The American luxury liners were heavily subsidized, and the British-owned Union Royal Mail suffered severely from the American competition. British shipping interests and Australian and New Zealand seamen's unions and newspapers soon launched a concerted campaign against the Matson line, demanding that the Dominion governments take action to exclude the line from the trans-Tasman service. Characteristic of the editorial comments were those of the Melbourne *Age:*

> The carefully organized American invasion of inter-Dominion shipping trade calls for immediate co-operative action in self-defence by the Governments of Australia and New Zealand. . . . As Americans never tire of preaching, a nation's chief duty is to attend to its own welfare. The welfare of this country and New Zealand certainly will not be promoted by tamely submitting to American monopolisation of Pacific Ocean traffic.[13]

Public opinion in Australia and New Zealand strongly supported the agitation against the Matson line, but two factors prevented governmental action. New Zealand built up a thriving tourist trade soon after Matson added Auckland as a port of call, and this trade would disappear if Auckland were again by-passed. Officials of the Matson company made it known that if excluded from the inter-Dominion service, they would cease calling at Auckland. New Zealand thus had much to lose if restrictive legislation were adopted. An even more important consideration that deterred government action was the influence of the British government. Britain had long opposed restrictive shipping legislation and with good reason. In the early 1930's Britain controlled over ninety per cent of the Empire trade, almost sixty per cent of the trade between the Empire and foreign ports, and about twenty-five per cent of the trade between non-British countries. Restrictions designed to assure even more of the Empire trade would only bring retaliation causing loss of trade in the other two categories.[14]

Washington was aware that London opposed action against the Matson line, for in October, 1932, Prime Minister Lyons told the Australian parliament that the issue had been discussed at Ottawa and that the home government had advised caution.[15] Three years later the British government yielded to pressure from the Peninsular and Oriental steamship company, which controlled the Union line, and withdrew opposition to restrictive legislation; and when the United States government learned of this development it took vigorous action to get London to reassert its influence. The Commercial Counselor of the British embassy, Harry O. Chalkley, was called to the State Department and told that action against the Matson line would bring an irresistible effort in the American Congress for restrictive legislation against British shipping.[16] This threat proved effective, at least for a time, for in the following months no action was taken by the Dominion governments. Not until 1937 did the Matson issue emerge again.

In addition to trade and shipping issues, strategic considerations also created dissension between Australia and the United States. A decisive development came in 1932 when the United States passed the Hawes-Cutting Act providing for Philippine independence after a ten-year transitional period. This policy, finally implemented with the Tydings-McDuffie Act in 1934, was resented by Australians. They interpreted it as an American withdrawal from the Western Pacific and therefore as a blow to Australian security. Ill-will was also generated by the Anglo-American controversy over cruiser strength. The refusal of the United States to agree to a substantial increase in British light cruiser strength at the London Naval Conference in 1930 was viewed by Australians as a serious threat to their defensive position.[17] With America's withdrawal from the Pacific and Britain's naval power impaired, Australians believed they were compelled to maintain good relations with Japan.

That many Australians regarded it necessary to conciliate Japan became evident during the Manchurian crisis of 1931-1933. Australian popular sentiment seemed to welcome Japan's thrust into Manchuria, since it appeared to lessen the chances of a Japanese advance to the south.[18] Though some Australian newspapers criticized Japan's invasion, many were noncommittal or avowedly pro-Japanese.[19] Australians favored a policy even more moderate than that initially pursued in 1931 by Secretary of State Henry L. Stimson; and when in early 1932 Stimson abandoned conciliation in favor of moral suasion and nonrecognition, the gap between Australian and United States policy widened. Although in March, 1932, Australia followed Britain in approving Stimson's nonrecognition doctrine, its approval was lacking in enthusiasm. Had it become known in Canberra that at times Stimson urged upon Hoover a policy of economic sanctions, Australian leaders would have grown alarmed. It is likely that Australia used its influence with the United Kingdom against just such a policy.[20] In 1935 during the naval conversations at London, the American delegate, Norman Davis, learned that Australia was at that time urging upon the British government a conciliatory policy.[21]

Reports from the American consulate general at Sydney confirmed the information regarding Australia's policy toward Japan. In 1935 Consul General Jay Pierrepont Moffat reported: "I have yet to meet an Australian who opposed Japan's Manchurian policy or desired to see Japan out of Manchuria."[22] In that same year Sir George Pearce, the Minister for External Affairs, told Moffat that Australia remained suspicious of Japan's ultimate intentions but with British naval strength reduced below the safety point and with American aid discounted, no policy was open other than to try to be friendly to Japan, to give her no excuse to adopt an aggressive policy toward Australia, and to rejoice every time Japan advanced more deeply into Manchukuo.[23] In 1936, a time when Australians were becoming more and more worried about Japanese aggression, Moffat reported "an increasing bitterness at our policy of withdrawal from the Philippines."[24]

CHAPTER TWO

Australia Takes the Road
to Economic Autarchy

I$_N$ 1933 the economic paths of the United States and Australia diverged. In the United States Franklin D. Roosevelt became President and named as his Secretary of State Cordell Hull of Tennessee, a man dedicated to the revival of international trade through the lowering of tariffs. Hull viewed the re-establishment of world trade and the reassertion of traditional principles of morality as the prescription for all the world's ills, both economic and political. Though his doctrinaire approach proved woefully inadequate to meet the world problems of the 1930's, Hull remained constant in his attachment to this simple formula for world security and economic prosperity. To Hull the restoration of trade was almost a religion. His program to remove restrictions on world trade was soon to collide head-on with Australia's trade diversion policy.

When Roosevelt and Hull came into office in 1933, Lyons had been prime minister in Australia for just over a year. The Labour government of James Henry Scullin, which had been in office during most of the depression era, had been rent asunder in 1931 by a bitter dispute between the right and the left over plans for economic recovery. Scullin, a kindly, religious man, proved unequal to the task of holding his party together. The militant Labourite J. T. Lang led a leftist revolt, while Lyons headed a group that split off the right. When the Scullin ministry collapsed in January, 1932, Lyons assumed the Prime Ministry at the head of a new nonlabour United Australia party. Lyons, a man of quiet humility who had been a schoolteacher before entering politics as a Labour member of the Assembly in Tasmania, was regarded by many as a stopgap

12

prime minister, but he was destined to remain in office until his death in 1939—a period of seven years, three months, and one day, a record previously exceeded only by the pugnacious William Morris Hughes whose term was twelve days longer.

During the first two years of the Lyons ministry, Australia made significant progress in pulling out of the economic depression. In the process, however, the Ottawa Agreement and individual tariff bills had raised imperial preference margins to new heights. As a result Australia built up considerable resentment among European countries that traded heavily with Australia and usually had an unfavorable balance of trade with Australia. By early 1934 Australia was beginning to feel pressure: continental countries demanded that Australia either import more products from them or export less to them. Rather than reduce imperial preference margins, however, the Australian government turned to what appeared to be an easier solution. It undertook to completely overhaul United States-Australian trade relations in order to eliminate the roughly six-to-one unfavorable balance of trade.

On June 4, 1934, Prime Minister Lyons presented to Consul General John K. Caldwell a list of Australian trade requests that was so sweeping and extraordinary that it generated something akin to incredulity in Washington. Australia demanded free entry annually of a "reasonable amount" of wool, fifty thousand tons of butter, ten thousand tons of beef and a like amount of mutton and lamb, the amounts to be increased when Australia could supply more. The Australian proposal also requested the United States to restrict its own exports of apples and dried fruits to Europe and the British Commonwealth in order to leave the market open for Australian exports.[1]

When the June 4 proposal was telegraphed to Washington, former Prime Minister Stanley M. Bruce, now High Commissioner to the United Kingdom, was visiting in the United States, and on June 6 Assistant Secretary of State Francis B. Sayre took up the issue with Bruce, hoping to secure a clarification of the Australian démarche. Bruce explained that there had been overproduction in Australia and that other countries were threatening to restrict Australian imports. Australia therefore deemed it necessary to attempt to redress the unfavorable balance of trade with the United States. He conceded that any attempt to balance trade between individual countries was "nonsense," but, he insisted, the situation of Australia was not a happy one and these factors, however unsound economically, had to be given consideration. He admitted that the United States produced the same products as Australia and that a trade agreement would entail certain difficulties for the United States, but, he said, it would boost Australia tremendously if the United States could buy more Australian products.[2]

Before replying to the June 4 proposal, Secretary Hull sent it to the chairman of the Tariff Commission, Robert L. O'Brien. The Commissioner's views reinforced the opinions that were already being aired in the State Department. O'Brien advised Hull that the importation of the Australian products in the amounts proposed would completely upset the market conditions that the Agricultural Adjustment Administration was attempting to stabilize. Regarding the request that the United States limit its own exports in favor of Australian products, O'Brien said that such a proposal was to his knowledge "unexampled in commercial negotiations."[3] O'Brien and Hull agreed that only one reply could be sent to Australia, an unqualified no.

Before the American rejection was dispatched to Australia, Hull's own program for lowering trade barriers was approved by Congress with the passage of the Reciprocal Trade Agreements Act. A new framework was thus constructed within which United States-Australian trade discussions would take place. The bill empowered the executive to negotiate with other governments agreements lowering (by as much as fifty per cent) the existing rates on imports from those countries, or freezing existing rates or import restrictions, in return for reciprocal concessions on American products imported into the foreign countries. Though public notice and hearings were required, the executive had full power to conclude the treaties, and no action either by the Senate or the Congress as a whole was required to put them into effect. The Act also contained a directive that the agreements embody the most-favored-nation principle in its unconditional form. This meant that when an agreement with one country lowered the duties on certain imports, the same reduction took effect on such goods imported from other countries, provided only that the countries in question did not discriminate against the trade of the United States. Thus each agreement had the effect of lowering duties on a wide front, not just between the two parties to the pact.[4]

Hull's rejection of the June 4 proposal, presented to Prime Minister Lyons in January, 1935, explained the reciprocal trade program in detail. In the course of the analysis one fact was clear: the Australian approach to trade problems was diametrically opposed to Hull's program. "Far from diverting trade from one country to another," he said, "this program has as its chief purpose the opening up of world trade by lessening generally the obstacles to trade." It would leave trade balances to be effected "in the natural roundabout fashion as in the past." Hull then said that the United States must begin this program by negotiations with countries whose products were not so directly competitive with its own. Hull conceded that Australia would gain little from the indirect benefits in the early stages because the first negotiations would not cover many items exported by Australia, but he expressed the hope that there might later be found a better basis for negotiating on the more competitive products.[5]

When the American rejection was received, Sir Henry Gullett, Minister in Charge of Trade Negotiations, observed that it was "not altogether unexpected."[6] The Australian proposal was so unrealistic that it was doomed from its inception. This was so clearly the case that many Australian officials had opposed the project. Years later Chargé d'Affaires John R. Minter learned that almost all civil servants connected with Australia's overseas trade policy had opposed the dispatch of the note, even the Comptroller General of Customs.[7] Frank Murphy, Secretary in the Department of Commerce, who along with Arthur C. Moore had drafted the proposal, was reported even to have expressed regret for his part in drafting the proposals. The move had indeed been a serious mistake. For almost a decade after the June 4 proposal the Department of State scanned with a suspicious eye all Australian proposals, and the Department persisted in the opinion that the Australian government was one which asked for everything and offered nothing in return.

As ill-advised as the June 4 proposal was and as ill-informed as Australian leaders were when they submitted it, in the months that followed those same leaders were shrewdly accurate in their assessment of Hull's trade program as it related to Australia. However grand Hull's principles, however sincere his devotion to those principles, Australian officials discerned that his reciprocal trade program offered no substantial benefit to Australia. Though Hull sought to lower tariffs on a broad front, he could do nothing with agricultural products. The Roosevelt administration had undertaken a gigantic and costly program to restore farm income through price support, acreage reduction, and destruction of livestock, and the President could not approve tariff concessions that would damage that program. A reduction in the wool tariff could probably have been justified economically, but both Roosevelt and Hull knew that the political aspects of the question could not be ignored. The reciprocal trade program had been authorized for only three years, and Hull lived in almost constant fear that the Congress would not renew it in 1937. If the opposition of the wool-growing states were added to the opposition which already existed, the whole program might be ended.

The Roosevelt administration thus could do little to aid Australia in matters of trade, and it sought to improve relations through less costly ways. When Prime Minister and Mrs. Lyons visited Washington on their way home from London in 1935, Roosevelt invited them to be his guests in the White House, and every effort was exerted to make their visit enjoyable. In addition to talking with Roosevelt, Lyons conferred with Hull. Though the Secretary of State could offer nothing substantial, he was generous with praise for the likeable, tousle-haired Prime Minister. Hull, using some homespun psychology, said he was glad to be one of Lyon's followers "in this righteous movement back towards economic sanity and economic rehabilitation generally." Such praise must have sounded strange to the Prime Minister of a country which was rapidly moving toward bilateral bartering agreements and manipulation of trade balances. Lyons was scarcely an appropriate candidate for the leader of the forces fighting autarchy. He took it all in stride, however, and returned to Australia with a more kindly regard for the United States than was current among his ministerial colleagues.[8]

Shortly after Lyons returned home, Roosevelt sought to improve relations with Australia in still another way. He sent to the consulate general at Sydney one of the State Department's top young diplomats, Jay Pierrepont Moffat. At the time of his appointment to the Sydney post, Moffat had been serving for two years as Chief of the Division of Western European Affairs, the desk that handled all matters relating to Western Europe and the entire British Commonwealth. Harvard-educated, handsome and urbane, Moffat was ideally suited for a post which Roosevelt wished to elevate in importance. Moffat was glad to receive the Sydney assignment because, as he wrote to his father-in-law Ambassador Joseph C. Grew at Tokyo, "There is real political work to be done."[9] The consulate general at Sydney now superseded the British embassy at Washington as the principal channel of communication with Australia. It became a quasi-legation, and until ministers were exchanged in 1940 it performed all the duties of a regular diplomatic mission, though it lacked the rank and—much to the remorse of the consuls general—the budget of a legation.

The hoped-for improvement in United States-Australian relations did not occur. On the contrary, the long-smoldering resentment in Australia over the unfavorable balance of trade soon ignited into governmental action to restrict American trade. During late 1935 and early 1936 Consul General Moffat watched anxiously as events moved toward a crisis. In October, 1935, he had a long conference with Sir George Pearce, the Minister for External Affairs, a man whom Moffat characterized as a "slow-spoken, kindly eyed, elderly gentleman, who had the gift of saying some pretty bitter things without giving offense." Sir George recited at length Australia's complaints against the United States—the refusal to join the League, the checking of Britain's cruiser strength, the withdrawal from the Philippines, and the unfavorable balance of trade. He told Moffat frankly that something had to be done, and done soon, to improve the trade balance, or Australia would be compelled to take measures to limit American imports.[10] Moffat also talked with other leaders at Canberra. "One and all," he reported to Hull, "spoke with varying degrees of bitterness about Australia's adverse trade balance with the United States."[11]

Prime Minister Lyons was not eager to take action against the United States, but he was suffering from increasing political embarrassment as public sentiment against American trade grew. Lyons literally pleaded with Moffat for some concession that might appease the Australian public. Could the United States not do something, make some gesture, give some unilateral concession—anything to help him in meeting the attack on American trade which would come when Parliament convened? Moffat could offer nothing, but at the request of Lyons he sent the Prime Minister's appeal to Hull for his personal attention.[12]

Lyons soon found himself caught not only in a political squeeze but in an economic bind as well. In the first months of 1936 Australia experienced a mild economic boom, but, instead of improving, Australia's financial situation worsened. The prosperity caused imports to escalate to dangerous proportions while exports gained only slightly. As a result Australia had to draw heavily upon her London funds to meet overseas obligations. By March, 1936, Australia teetered on the brink of a financial crisis. On March 4 Sir Henry Gullett telephoned Moffat from Melbourne to describe the desperate situation of the government and to urge the opening of trade negotiations. Gullett warned that the pressure on the government to restrict American trade was growing in proportion as Australia's balance of payments became increasingly precarious.[13]

On March 14 Moffat met with Gullett to give him Hull's long-awaited reply to Lyons' appeal of October, 1935. It was the same answer as was previously received from Washington: a treaty could not be negotiated at this time.[14] Gullett's disappointment was keen, and he confided to Moffat that the Australian government would almost certainly take measures to restrict American trade. The cabinet had already discussed such steps, he explained, and the pressure from Parliament was growing more and more difficult to resist. There was an instinctive disinclination to take measures against the United States, partly because of her attempt to do something in trade on a broad and constructive line, and partly because of the wish to keep on the best terms with the United States with the worsening of conditions in Europe and the Pacific. These important considerations, however, paled into insignificance, said Gullett, before the vital and immediate task of maintaining Australia's financial credit.[15]

In early April matters took an ominous turn. In a parliamentary debate on April 1, government supporters exhibited great bitterness at the extent of American imports, and the ministry was accused of weakness in dealing with the United States. ". . . we cannot overlook the fact," said Representative Archie Cameron, "that the policy it [the United States] applies is 'Everything for the United States of America and nothing for the other fellow.' "[16] The tone of the debate so alarmed Moffatt that he telegraphed Hull asking him to send a message to Lyons that would dispel the belief that America was indifferent to the welfare of Australia.[17] Hull immediately replied, but he could only repeat the same old arguments and then urge Australia to join with the United States in the fight for a liberal commercial policy.[18] The message had not the slightest impact on the developments in Australia, as Washington must have anticipated. By early May the Lyons ministry was drawing up plans for a comprehensive trade diversion program.

The government's emerging policy, though doubtless popular, did not enjoy unanimous support. Many newspapers, including the *Morning Herald,* the *Labour Daily,* the *Telegraph,* and the *Sun,* all of Sydney, the *Argus* and the *Herald* of Melbourne cautioned the government against precipitate action. The press pointed out that it would be suicidal for Australia to antagonize the United States at the very moment that the outlook for peace in Europe and the Far East was so problematical.[19] An incisive criticism was also leveled on the floor of the House of Representatives. Sir Donald Cameron reminded the members of the House that if Australia took steps to balance its trade with the United States, it might put ideas into the heads of other nations with whom Australia had favorable balances of trade. He went on to reiterate the anxiety manifested by the press. "The United States of America," he observed, "is a Pacific power whose co-operation may be vitally and urgently needed in circumstances which it is easier to imagine than to state, and which it would be inadvisable to particularize."[20]

The injunctions to caution were in vain. On May 20 Moffat noted in his diary: "The sword of Damocles is about to fall."[21] Two days later it fell. On the afternoon of May 22 the government tabled a new and drastic tariff schedule. The list substantially increased rates on many items on the general tariff schedule of which the United States was the predominant supplier. Textiles were also raised drastically, thus dealing a serious blow to Japan. A second phase of the program was directed almost exclusively against the United States. The importation of a long list of items from countries outside the British Empire was prohibited except under licenses. The list included motor chassis, motorcycles, typewriters, household applicances, metal-working machinery, iron and steel sheets and plates, and many other items usually obtained from the

United States.[22] Most of the benefits of the new program would accrue to the United Kingdom. Of the £ 2,290,000 the government estimated would be diverted, Australian manufacturers were expected to benefit by £ 845,000, good customer foreign countries by £ 135,000 and the United Kingdom by £ 1,310,000.[23]

Moffat estimated that the items on the prohibited list constituted about twenty per cent of American trade, by value about £ 2,000,000. The Australian government planned to issue licenses freely for imports from countries with which Australia had a favorable balance of trade. From other countries, particularly the United States, licenses would be granted only when it was to Australia's interest. In the case of automobile chassis, a major item in the American trade, licenses would be issued for imports from the United States during the year ending April 30, 1937, equal to the number imported during the year ending April 30, 1936. The government's decision to allow this trade to continue was dictated by the fear of bringing chaos to the Australian plants dependent upon American chassis. Typewriters from the United States were put on a quota basis of seventy-five per cent of the previous year's imports, but no other items on the prohibited list were to be imported from the United States unless unprocurable elsewhere at greatly increased cost.[24]

The licensing system was a clear case of discrimination against the United States. "The Government has not only discriminated against us," Moffat reported, "but exulted in it."[25] Hull sent a protest deploring the Australian action, and when Moffat delivered it, he gained some revealing insights into Australian motives.

Pearce, the Minister for External Affairs, frankly admitted that the policy was drastic, discriminatory, and even dangerous. Nevertheless, he observed, the measure was perhaps the most popular one with members of Parliament of any introduced by the Lyons ministry. Ten years ago, he said, no ministry could have taken such action against the United States and survived six months, but America's policy and her attitude with regard to trade had now brought relations to such a pass. When Moffat asked if Pearce saw any "ray of light," Pearce replied that perhaps after the November elections in the United States the Department of State would be willing to negotiate. Here was a clear signal that Australia intended to use the discriminations to force concessions from Washington. Moffat was keenly aware that the Department would take great offense at the employment of such a tactic by Australia, and he proceeded to warn Pearce of this. He said he hoped Australia was not misgauging American psychology and thinking that pressure would facilitate negotiations. "We do seem to be getting involved," conceded Pearce, but he thought the big nation should extend the olive branch to the smaller one even though the latter had offended.[26]

Pearce's candor was not apparent in the formal reply which Australia sent to the American protest. This communication, drafted by Gullett and Richard G. Casey, the Treasurer, maintained the fiction that the Australian policy was not discriminatory.[27] Washington doubtless found it difficult to reconcile Pearce's frank admission of discrimination with the disclaimers in the formal reply submitted over his name. The Department of State accepted the candid version. It could do little else. The diversion program was so obviously discriminatory that Hull and his associates could not arrive at a different conclusion even if they wished to do so. Immediate steps were taken to withdraw from Australia the lower tariff rates which she received indirectly through America's reciprocal trade treaties with other countries. Under the Reciprocal Trade Act these benefits accrued to all nations which did not discriminate against American trade, and Australia could no longer be numbered among that group. In June Washington sent word to Canberra that beginning August 1 the benefits under the trade agreements legislation would be withdrawn.[28]

The trade diversion program was destined to be a political asset to the Lyons ministry for many months, yet the inherent weaknesses of the system were so apparent that the policy was criticized throughout its duration. The Labour opposition especially was critical of the policy. John Curtin, leader of the Labour party, stated that the government would have been wiser to avoid national discrimination and that political as well as economic repercussions seemed almost inevitable.[29] The *Labour Daily* on May 25, 1936, attacked the reckless action of the ministry in declaring a trade war on the two most powerful nations in the Pacific, the United States and Japan. The diversion program, said the Labour organ,

> follows so closely upon the visits of Lord Nuffield, the British motor-car manufacturer, and the Manchester Trade Delegation, that it would appear as if Australia's future has been jeopardized in order to meet

the demands of the imperialists that the Australian market should become a closed preserve for British manufacturers.[30]

The Lyons ministry was particularly vulnerable to its detractors because of the measures taken against Japan. Politically their actions meant the abandonment of the conciliatory policy which the government had been pursuing since 1931. Though the validity of that moderate policy was itself questionable, Australia had now cancelled out any benefits she might have derived from it. Economically the restrictions on Japanese imports were also open to criticism. Japan had contributed significantly to Australia's recovery during 1929-1933, having doubled her total imports of raw wool during that period. During 1933-1934 Japan took twenty per cent of Australia's wool exports.[31] These heavy purchases resulted in a very favorable balance of trade for Australia. This fact was a source of considerable embarrassment to the Lyons ministry as it attempted to explain the theory of trade diversion. If the purpose of the policy was to divert trade from Australia's "bad customers" to her "good customers," as the ministry alleged, why was Japan, an extremely "good customer," singled out for discrimination by high duties on textiles?

The trade diversion program manifestly had other objectives than to solve the foreign exchange problem. It was a comprehensive system to benefit British commercial interests. Japan was a "good customer," but she was also a keen competitor of British textile interests in the Australian market. In 1934 Japan had replaced Britain as the largest supplier of textiles to Australia. In an attempt to check this influx of cheap goods, the Australian government had opened negotiations with Japan in 1935 hoping to secure a voluntary agreement to restrict imports from Japan. When in May, 1936, these discussions reached an impasse, British textile interests succeeded in persuading the government to place high tariffs on Japanese goods as part of the trade diversion program.[32]

Unlike the United States, Japan quickly took decisive retaliatory action against the diversion program. In June, 1936, the Tokyo government prohibited the importation of Australian wool, wheat, and flour, except under license. High tariff duties were imposed on other items coming from Australia. The Australian licensing system was then extended to almost all goods coming from Japan, virtually halting trade between the two countries.[33] As the months passed, it became apparent that Australia had grossly underestimated Japan's ability to free herself from dependence on Australian wool. Though she had formerly secured eighty-five to ninety-five per cent of her wool from Australia, Japan now turned successfully to New Zealand, South Africa, and other areas. She also embarked upon a program to free herself from dependence on Australia by developing staple fiber substitutes. Thus the voices of Australian wool growers added to the clamor of the Labour party opposition to the diversion program.[34] In December a stop-gap agreement was negotiated with Japan, but Australia was never to regain her former position in the Japanese market.[35]

Among the public and even among exporters in the United States no great reaction to the Australian measures was discernible. John R. Minter, who handled the Australian desk at the Department of State, wrote Moffat: "No one seems to be very unhappy over the prospect of losing a small percentage of his trade or of only being able to ship an amount equal to that shipped in the previous twelve months:"[36] American officials, however, were indignant over the matter. When Premier Bertram Stevens of New South Wales called on Hull in August, 1936, the Secretary inveighed against the cutthroat economic bilateralism and autarchy still prevalent in the rest of the world. He was amazed, he said, that "our Australian friends . . . are putting a knife to our throats."[37]

Despite the large tide of resentment running against Australia at the State Department, Hull decided upon a policy of "watchful waiting." The withdrawal of benefits under the reciprocal trade program was not calculated to bring Australia to terms, for Australia had anticipated and discounted that step.[38] It was believed, however, that eventually the British home government would exert its influence against the diversion program. Initially Moffat did not share Washington's confidence, for he considered that "in matters of trade London is bitterly hostile."[39] Within a few months, however, Moffat learned that the home government had not given its blessing to the diversion program. In a conversation with a high official of the Governor General's office in Australia, Moffat found that that office had received a copy of the diversion program only twenty-four hours or so before it was tabled.[40]

In February, 1937, Moffat learned that Prime Minister Neville Chamberlain gave a direct snub to Minister for Commerce Earle

Page when it was hinted that Australia's diversion program should entitle her to more favorable consideration in Anglo-Australian trade negotiations. It would not make "one whit of difference" the Prime Minister had stated emphatically. About that same time McClure-Smith, the editor of the Sydney *Morning Herald,* told Moffat that he was surprised how many people believed that Whitehall had inspired the trade diversion policy, when, as a matter of fact, he knew that it had embarrassed the Foreign Office and perhaps other sections of the government.[41]

The belief at Washington that Britain did not approve of the diversion program—a belief Moffat came to share—was well founded. Britain was at this very time preparing to take the first steps toward a rapprochement with the United States and seriously considering bringing her trade program into line with Hull's movement to free international trade. The unexpected Australian move cut across the home government's plans. Many years later Page revealed in his memoirs just how coolly news of the diversion program was received in London. When the information arrived, both Page and Attorney General Robert Menzies were in London, and they went together to give the "good news" to Lord Runciman at the Board of Trade. "He certainly failed to show that extraordinary pleasure we anticipated," Page later recorded. Menzies' comment to Page after the meeting perhaps summed up the episode best: "You offered him a present of from ten to twenty million pounds in Australian trade, and he looked as though you'd kicked him in the stomach."[42]

Hull and his associates hoped from the outset that Britain would help end the diversion program. In October, 1936, James C. Dunn, occupying Moffat's former post as Chief of the Division of Western European Affairs, sent Moffat a full explanation of the Department's hopes for British support. After first noting that Hull was reluctant to bring the Australian matter up in controversial form, as it might adversely affect the reciprocal trade program, he went on to discuss the London aspect of the question:

> As we come closer to grips with this entire situation, we have in mind bringing up the Australian difficulties either directly on the basis of the general situation or possibly enlisting also the help of the British Government if and when we come to the point where the British will really put their shoulders to the wheel with us in support of

the entire program. We know now that the British Government have already urged through their representatives in countries of the so-called Sterling group, that is, the Scandinavian countries and Argentina, the modification of exchange restrictions and the freeing generally of international trade, and we feel that we may soon find them, that is, the British, working with us in the advancement of the general restoration of international trade.

This picture, as I give it to you, may explain somewhat the lack of action or reaction from here, to which may be added the fact that we do not know exactly how we could ever give even a measure of satisfaction to the Australians through the negotiation of a trade agreement.[43]

The United States made two attempts to invoke the aid of Britain in 1936, but the British were not yet ready to "really put their shoulders to the wheel." In July the State Department sounded Harry O. Chalkley, the Commercial Counselor of the British Embassy, and Chalkley said it was a matter into which they did not want to be drawn.[44] Then in October Ambassador Robert W. Bingham was instructed to request support from Foreign Secretary Anthony Eden. Eden pleaded lack of information and later sent a noncommittal reply.[45] Despite these rebuffs, the Department remained convinced that British aid would be forthcoming.

Early in 1937 reports from Moffat at Sydney reinforced Washington's hopes that its moderate policy would ultimately be successful. In January Richard G. Casey, the Treasurer, told Moffat that it was absolutely necessary that the British Empire and the United States compose their differences *en grand*. From this conversation and others, Moffat discerned "a distinct change of atmosphere and a growing recognition that the trade diversion policy as at present drawn up must ultimately be altered." "I can't help wondering," Moffat noted in his diary, "whether Eden, even though refusing Bingham's request to help him, none the less dropped a few hints to Mr. Bruce."[46] By February the indications were even more definite. Attorney General Robert G. Menzies, whom Moffat believed was daily pulling more weight in the cabinet, told Moffat that a mistake had been made and that it never could have occurred had he not been absent in London.[47] In March came another encouraging development. Sir Henry Gullett—the "archpriest of bilateral balancing" in Moffat's view—resigned from the cabinet when some of his trade negotiations came under fire. "This will immeasurably facilitate the ultimate solution of our troubles," Moffat noted in his diary.[48]

The indications were heartening. Moffat nevertheless realized that there was no chance of immediate reconsideration of the diversion program. Within a short time Lyons and other leaders would leave for the Imperial Conference in London. Moffat was hopeful, however, that after the conference something might be accomplished. Though Moffat had on occasion evidenced some impatience with the Department of State's moderate policy, he now fully concurred with the policy of "watchful-waiting." "Time is on our side," he reported to the Department; "the trend of opinion is at last moving slowly in the right direction; but it is not yet ripe for forcing a change. I feel that our best tactics are to let matters develop without further moves by us until after the Imperial Conference."[49] With these views Washington wholeheartedly agreed.

CHAPTER THREE

1937: A Year of Cross-Currents

THE world order established by the Versailles treaty was crumbling rapidly by the beginning of 1937. The ineffective sanctions against Italy during the Ethiopian invasion in 1935-1936 had revealed the League of Nations' impotence to the entire world. Hitler's march into the demilitarized Rhineland in 1936 had struck another blow at the status quo. In the Far East signs indicated that Japan might expand her conquests beyond Manchuria and Jehol province, where the tide of expansion had stopped in 1933. In Japan itself the military and patriotic groups had so intimidated the civilian leaders by assassinations and incidents—the latest being the incident of February 26, 1936, when troops held Tokyo for three days in defiance of the government—that the military could virtually dictate the policies of the government. With England threatened in Europe and with war imminent in the Far East, Canberra had little choice but to begin a reappraisal—hesitant though it was—of her relations with the United States, no matter how small the chance of help from that isolationist quarter might be.

While international developments were beginning to influence United States-Australian relations, the old issues of trade and shipping continued to foment antagonism. The new forces working to bring the countries together thus contended with the old divisive forces in a confused and illogical pattern. Late in 1936 the Matson issue emerged again, bringing more ill-will. Shortly thereafter the Australian government appointed a liaison officer to Washington, a step which seemed to point to closer diplomatic cooperation. All the while the trade diversion policy continued to generate ill feeling. If any further development were needed to produce cross-currents in United States-Australian relations in 1937, it was provided by

27

Prime Minister Lyons' proposal for a Pacific pact that would unite Australia in a nonaggression arrangement with Japan and possibly the United States, the two countries against whom Australia had declared a trade war in 1936.

The Matson issue revived suddenly in October, 1936, when the New Zealand government decided to take action. A bill, which had as its objective the excluding of the Matson line from the trans-Tasman trade, was introduced in the Parliament on October 22 by the Minister of Marine, Peter Fraser. Later the same evening the Australian government announced that it would soon follow New Zealand's lead and introduce parallel legislation.[1] The next day the British ambassador at Washington, Sir Ronald Lindsay, transmitted a note from the New Zealand government setting forth its position on the Matson issue.

The New Zealand legislation, passed a few days later, outlawed Tasman traffic to ships of a country receiving subsidies that enabled them to compete on unequal terms with British shipping. The bill was also designed to open the Hawaii-San Francisco trade to Britain, from which it had been excluded by American coastwise shipping legislation. In addition to the provision on subsidies, the bill outlawed Tasman traffic to ships of a country that prohibited British ships from carrying passengers or goods between ports of that country and its territories. The legislation was framed so that it could be used as a bargaining card before its implementation. Its provisions would not automatically come into force but could be administered at any time by an Order in Council. The New Zealand government announced that this enabling legislation would not be applied until the United States had an opportunity to comment, and the Australian Minister of Commerce likewise intimated that the United States would be given a last opportunity to admit British shipping to the Hawaii-San Francisco trade.[2]

In the face of this legislation, the American government did not retreat from its position. John R. Minter of the Division of Western European Affairs advised Hull:

> The New Zealand note calls for only one kind of reply from us, to wit, an expression of disapproval of all the thoughts and principles underlying the note and the legislation to which it refers both as to their meaning and their motive, and an emphatic statement that we are not prepared to negotiate either regarding our coasting trade or the amounts of subsidies which any line may be granted.

Minter was so fearful of the repercussions from the New Zealand note and the American reply, if these exchanges became known, that he urged Hull to ask Lindsay to withdraw the note. The reply which the Department must send, said Minter, would lend encouragement to the "very powerful interests" in the United States which had long sought to establish policies of discrimination in favor of American shipping.[3]

When Hull conferred with the British ambassador on October 28 he requested that the note be withdrawn. He also pointed out the serious danger of retaliatory legislation and said he could not assume that the British government was proposing to embark upon a policy of coastwise shipping throughout the Empire and among its independent communities. When Lindsay protested that this indeed was not the British policy, Hull made an adroit thrust at British acquiescence. When such a communication was transmitted for New Zealand without any adverse comment by the government at London, said Hull, certain inferences could be drawn. The British government was doubtless embarrassed by the issue. A few days later Lindsay, having consulted London, agreed to withdraw the note and consider the contents to have been conveyed orally.[4]

The American government could afford to take a firm stand, for it held the high cards. Britain had more to lose by a policy of discriminatory shipping restrictions than had any country in the world. New Zealand, the Dominion now taking the lead in the Matson dispute, also had much to lose. If the enabling legislation were implemented, it was predictable that Matson would drop Auckland as a port of call, thus diverting a thriving tourist trade from New Zealand to Australia. The Auckland *Star* noted on October 23: "Why should the Government of the Dominion which has most to lose by the contemplated action take the lead?" The *Star* also saw some justice in the American position regarding the Hawaiian trade. "It would be difficult in any event to convince the Americans," it stated, "that Australia and New Zealand, which have been repeatedly declared to be autonomous, self-governing communities, should for the purpose of this shipping dispute, be considered as one country in the same sense as the United States and Hawaii."

Of all the countries involved in the dispute, Australia had the least to lose, and there the reserving of the Tasman trade was extremely popular.[5] In December, 1936, while the trade controversy with the United States was at its height, the Australian government introduced in the Parliament an enabling bill similar to the New Zealand legislation, but various developments delayed action on the legislation. On the same afternoon the bill was introduced the press took up for the first time a lively discussion of the crisis leading to the abdication of Edward VIII, and the press was so monopolized with this new issue that the Matson case was completely eclipsed. The Australian government was perhaps relieved at this cessation of public agitation on the issue, for in the succeeding weeks it was in no hurry to push the measure through. News of Washington's reaction to the New Zealand note doubtless had an influence on the Australian government. In any case the Parliament postponed debate on the measure until it would reassemble in the following year.[6] In New Zealand meanwhile no steps were taken to implement the legislation which had been enacted. Thus a showdown on the Matson issue was again postponed.

It is likely that the British home government exerted the controlling influence throughout the Matson dispute. There is reason to believe that by the end of 1936 the British government was beset with serious misgivings about the green light which it had given the Dominions and was attempting again to check them.

Before the Matson dispute emerged again to harass United States-Australian relations in the summer of 1937, a significant change took place in the diplomatic channel of communication. Since 1934 almost all negotiations had been handled through the consul general in Australia. Now, in 1937, two developments shifted the channel of communication back to Washington. First, Moffat was transferred back to Washington. While he was on leave in the United States in the summer of 1937, the Division of Western European Affairs was enlarged into the Division of European Affairs, and he was appointed the new Chief. With his continuing interest in Australia, Moffat and his associate John R. Minter, who had long managed Australian affairs in the Western European division, would now have the strongest voice in the formulation of policy.[7] A second development also tended to veer the channel of communication back to Washington: the appointment of an Australian liaison officer to the British embassy at Washington.

The appointment of an Australian diplomat to Washington was one manifestation of a growing Australian concern over external affairs. In 1935 the Ministry for External Affairs, previously attached to the Prime Minister's Department or the Attorney General's Office, was created a separate department with independent cabinet rank.[8] Then in November, 1936, Minister for External Affairs Pearce announced that the government had decided to embark on a policy of appointing officials abroad who would have diplomatic status. In February of the following year it was announced that an Australian counselor would be appointed to the British embassy in Washington. In May, 1937, F. Keith Officer, who had served since 1933 as the representative of the Department for External Affairs in London, was named to that post.

While Consul General in Australia, Moffat had constantly prodded the Australian government to open direct diplomatic relations with the United States, and he was largely responsible for this important new diplomatic connection. The Secretary of the Ministry for External Affairs, Lieutenant Colonel William R. Hodgson, told Moffat that the decision to send an Australian to Washington was chiefly the result of the views Moffat had continually expressed on the matter since his arrival in Australia. Moffat was somewhat disappointed that a fully accredited minister was not named, but several considerations had prevented such an appointment. The government was still debating the wisdom of sending ministers abroad. The appointment of a minister would also raise the difficult question of Tokyo. As Moffat noted in his diary: "The chief hitch had been a fear that the Japanese might take umbrage if the same thing weren't done in Tokyo, but it had been decided to introduce the measure as 'experimental.' I said [to Hodgson] that while it wasn't quite what I had hoped for, I was none the less delighted and felt Australia would never regret it."[9]

In actual practice the new position very nearly fulfilled Moffat's desires. Keith Officer's status soon developed into that of a quasi-minister. Though by the terms of his appointment he was a counselor to the British ambassador rather than a representative of the Australian government, he was referred to in Canberra as a "liaison officer."[10] Before long he was cabling communications to his government and conducting extensive conversations at the Department of State.

In the same month that the Australian liaison officer was appointed to Washington, another indication evidenced Australia's expanding interest in world affairs, particularly those relating to the Pacific. On May 22, 1937, at the Imperial Conference in London, Prime Minister Lyons presented a proposal for a Pacific pact. This suggestion was the culmination of Australia's interest in the Pacific area, an interest which had been growing since 1934. In that year Australia sent a good will mission to many of the countries of the Far East.[11] During 1934-1935 Trade Commissioners were named to New Zealand, Tokyo, Shanghai, and Batavia, and in 1937 these representatives were designated Government Commissioners.[12] As collective security disintegrated during 1936 and 1937 Australia turned to the concept of regional understandings in an attempt to offset the decline of the League. In proposals for the reform of the League Covenant put forward by Australia in 1936, it was suggested that the Covenant be reinforced by regional pacts of nonaggression, especially in the Pacific.[13] Then at the Imperial Conference in 1937 Lyons ventured his formal proposal for a Pacific pact.

The Lyons proposal came in the Prime Minister's opening speech to the Imperial Conference. Though Menzies and Pearce had discussed such a pact the previous September in the Australian Parliament, it now received much more publicity. Lyons suggested that the pact might be accepted by all countries of the Pacific and would have nonaggression and consultative provisions along the lines of the Four-Power Treaty of 1922. Unlike the treaty of 1922, however, the pact would not be limited to insular possessions but would provide for nonaggression generally in the Far East and the Pacific. The Australian proposal was referred to a committee, and when the committee made its report, the Imperial Conference agreed to the desirability of the proposal.[14] Whether the pact would materialize, however, depended largely upon the reaction of the other countries of the Pacific.

The Chinese government, facing the most immediate threat of aggression, seized upon the Lyons proposal with alacrity. The Chinese Minister of Finance, H. H. Kung, who was in London at the time of Lyons' speech, told William C. Bullitt, American ambassador to France, that China would be glad to enter into an agreement, not only for a nonaggression pact, but for treaties of mutual assistance.[15] In Tokyo the projected treaty was received with reticence and suspicion. Count Nobuaki Makino, Lord Keeper of the Privy Seal, frankly told the British ambassador that the time was not ripe for specific political agreements.[16] At Washington the reaction was cautious. "In giving this matter consideration," noted Stanley K. Hornbeck, Chief of the Far Eastern Division, "we should keep in mind the fact that Premier Lyons is making this subject a hobby and that certain Chinese officials are always enthusiastic over any kind of proposal which bids fair to bring about a commitment on the part of other powers to protect or to give China special assistance."[17] Within a few days, however, Hornbeck advocated wholehearted American support. He cautioned, though, that Britain should be allowed to take the initiative so as to avoid giving the Japanese the impression of collusion between the United States and Britain.[18] This policy was closely followed. When late in June Ambassador C. T. Wang of China urged the United States to declare itself favorably disposed to the Lyons proposal, Hornbeck told him that the matter was in the hands of the British and that the American government had "not adopted an attitude or position with regard to the matter."[19]

The British initiative on the Lyons proposal never materialized. Soon after the proposal was made, Chargé Ray Atherton at London gained the impression that the British were reluctant to proceed. The reasons were many. The British probably were disgruntled because no consultation occurred before the proposal was presented. British leaders also suspected, Atherton believed, that Lyons had made the proposal for political effect, the Australian general elections being scheduled for later in the year. There was also the difficult problem of what to do about Manchukuo, a subject which could hardly be avoided in any coming-to-terms in the Pacific area.[20] There was the further problem of America's long-standing policy of nonentanglement. Lyons assured Ambassador Bingham that he only hoped for a pact among the other powers which would receive "the blessing of the United States,"[21] but it is difficult to discern how the United States could have made a significant contribution to security on such a basis. Even if these considerations had not existed, however, Tokyo's veto of the project made its failure certain. If the only country which threatened the security of the Pacific could not be drawn into the nonaggression arrangement, nothing could be accomplished. By early July the pact proposal was virtually dead. It remained for the Japanese to give it the *coup de grâce* with the attack on China proper.

The first clash in the Sino-Japanese War on July 14, 1937, wrought a tremendous change in the milieu of United States-Australian relations. This fact was, however, only dimly appreciated at the time. So far as American records indicate, the outbreak of the war was not even a subject of discussion between Washington and Canberra, though that clash at Marco Polo Bridge was the beginning of a Pacific war which eventually engulfed both countries. The Sino-Japanese War thus had little immediate effect upon Australia's relations with the United States. The same could not be said regarding Australia's relations with Japan. The war initiated a fundamental reappraisal of Japan by the Australian government and people. Newspapers, which at the time of the Manchurian crisis had been noncommittal or pro-Japanese, now revealed outspoken hostility to Japan. Gone were the exultations over Japan's preoccupation on the continent.[22]

While Japanese armies were fanning out into North China, the United States and Australia were wrestling at Washington with the divisive issues which for years had warped the fabric of their relations. In June, 1937, the seemingly irrepressible Matson issue came up again. The bill to exclude Matson from the Tasman trade was still pending when the Parliament had reassembled after the Easter recess, and it had seemed likely that the measure would become law. As the weeks slipped by, however, the Lyons ministry betrayed no anxiety to get the measure passed. Instead the ministry decided to take up the matter with Washington again. In June Keith Officer delivered to the Department of State a detailed memorandum from the Australian government which repeated all the same arguments that had long been advanced—the exclusion of British shipping from the Hawaiian trade, the unfair competition resulting from the American subsidies.[23] This time the American government was in a position to make a more favorable reply to the Australian complaint. Under the provisions of the new Merchant Marine Act of 1936 the Matson subsidies were to end on June 30, 1937, two weeks later. The future subsidies provided for in the new legislation would be based solely upon operating differentials, and, according to Joseph P. Kennedy, the recently appointed Chairman of the Maritime Commission, they would not be excessive.[24]

The Australians were not appeased by the new American subsidy legislation, but the long-pending Matson issue nevertheless was soon to die. In August, Officer was still hinting that the Australian legislation would be passed,[25] but as the months went by the bill was not enacted. In New Zealand neither was anything done to implement the enabling legislation which had been adopted in October, 1936. The reasons for the demise of the issue are readily apparent. The lower American subsidies had an influence, though probably not a decisive one since the Union line was apparently more interested in breaking into the Hawaiian service than remedying the Tasman competition. New Zealand's fear of losing the tourist trade was a contributing factor. It seems virtually certain, however, that the most important deterrent was the influence of the British home government. Not only was British shipping too vulnerable to retaliation, but now there existed the even more compelling consideration: the desire for a general Anglo-American rapprochement. Thus the Matson issue which had plagued United States-Australian relations since 1931 finally disappeared amid the exigencies of a world spinning toward the holocaust.

CHAPTER FOUR

Ending Trade Diversion

W HEN the Australian delegation attended the Imperial Conference in 1937, it found that the Lyons proposal for a Pacific pact was not the only issue with a significant bearing on United States-Australian relations to be discussed at the conference. The subject of United States-Empire trade relations was also an important item pending before the conference, and this matter, with political as well as economic ramifications, was soon to have a far more profound effect upon United States-Australian relations than did the Lyons proposal.

In the fall of 1936 James C. Dunn, Chief of the Division of Western European Affairs, had informed Moffat that the United States hoped to utilize the aid of the British home government in ending the diversion policy "when we come to the point where the British will really put their shoulders to the wheel with us in support of the entire program." By the time of the Imperial Conference in 1937, the British had reached just that point. In 1936 the United States had opened conversations with Britain looking to the conclusion of a reciprocal trade agreement, and by early 1937 the British appeared to be ready to delve enthusiastically into the project. In doing so the British were no doubt motivated by broader considerations than by the possible trade benefits of a reciprocal trade treaty. Implicit in the development was England's strong desire for a general rapprochement with the United States.

The United States-United Kingdom trade talks raised difficult questions for England in her relations with the Dominions, for trade concessions to the United States would have to be made at the expense of imperial preference. Thus the Dominions, including Australia, would be intimately affected by the Anglo-American treaty.

36

It was necessary, therefore, that both England and the United States use their influence upon the Dominions to persuade them to make the necessary concessions regarding their preference in the United Kingdom market. At the Imperial Conference the United Kingdom government vigorously sought such support from the Dominions. At the close of the conference, Prime Minister Chamberlain made a very strong and moving impromptu appeal that the Dominions lend their cooperation to this project "which would mean so much."[1]

The Australian reaction both at home and at London was cautious and unenthusiastic. Trade Commissioner E. C. Squire at Sydney wrote Moffat: "The Australian press, particularly the S.M.H. [Sydney *Morning Herald*] has headlined the London soundings regarding an English-American trade (and political?) agreement. . . . Canberra reaction uneasy realizing British concessions would probably be at expense of some Australian preferences, for instance dried fruit."[2] Consul Albert M. Doyle, who was in charge of the consulate general pending the arrival of Moffat's successor, reported that the press carried voluminous dispatches from London regarding an Empire-United States trade pact and general rapprochement. "I get the impression," wrote Doyle, "that sentiment here is against any concessions to the U.S." Doyle also noted a fact which became increasingly evident during the U.S.-U.K. negotiations: "One can't avoid the impression that Great Britain is desperately anxious to get as close an understanding as possible with the U.S."[3]

The British appeal to the Dominions placed the Lyons ministry in an embarrassing dilemma. At the moment when Australia was engaged in a trade war with the United States and the Australian people were convinced that American trade deserved discriminations, England urged not discriminations—nor, indeed, merely an end to discriminations—but concessions. The timing was particularly unfortunate for the Lyons ministry, because elections were scheduled in Australia for later in the year. Lyons was thoroughly convinced that not only could he not grant concessions in the United Kingdom market before the elections, but he could not even reconsider the diversion policy until that hurdle was safely passed. It was doubtful that the diversion policy would at this stage gain votes for Lyons' party, but an acknowledgement by the ministry that it had been a mistake would certainly help the Labour opposition. Lyons was so concerned about the political overtones of the issue that he turned down an invitation to visit President Roosevelt on his way home, because he feared it would be interpreted as yielding ground to the United States. Such an appearance, Lyons confided to Ambassador Bingham at London, would be fatal to him and to his party.[4]

Throughout 1937 the Lyons ministry struggled to avoid the inevitable. The first tactic was delay. Lyons convinced United Kingdom leaders that nothing could possibly be done before the Australian elections. The State Department believed that Lyons struck a bargain with London officials whereby they would not embarrass him with pressure before the elections, provided he did not stick his neck out so far in speeches that he could not cooperate after the elections.[5] The Department soon learned definitely from Treasurer Richard G. Casey that Chamberlain had exacted a promise from Lyons that Australia would not be a stumbling block to successful negotiations with the United States.[6] Knowing this, Washington contented itself to wait out the elections. It could afford patience, for developments were moving decisively in its favor. England was earnestly seeking a rapprochement and—given Hull's strong feelings on matters of trade—there seemed no better step toward that objective than a reciprocal trade treaty. If the rapprochement required that Australia patch up her trade dispute with the United States and furthermore make sacrifices in the United Kingdom market, this would just have to be done.

There were two ways in which Washington might have eased Lyons' embarrassment. Concessions might have been granted to Australia either before or concurrent with Australia's abandonment of the diversion program. Washington, however, was in no mood to do this. Moreover, a vital principle was at stake. The Department had taken the position throughout the entire reciprocal trade program that it would not negotiate for the purpose of removing discriminations. A second alternative was open, though. The United States, while making no concessions until after the diversion program was ended, might have granted concessions to Australia before or concurrent with Australia's concessions in favor of the United States in the United Kingdom market. The United States also refused to consider this alternative. After months of Australian discrimination against American trade, Washington had little sympathy for Lyons' political embarrassment. There was also the more fundamental consideration that the United States expected the United Kingdom to make the necessary concessions to the Dominions. Thus Lyons was informed at the outset that the discrimination must end before the United States would even take up the subject of a trade treaty and that a satisfactory basis for a U.S.-U.K treaty must be struck before a United States-Australian treaty could be concluded.[7]

Conversations that took place during the visit of Treasurer Richard G. Casey to Washington in July, 1937, clearly highlighted the issues in Australian-American relations. On his way home from London he stopped by Washington and retraced the whole ground with governmental officials. Casey conferred with many high-ranking officers of the government, including Hull, but his most revealing conversation was that with Under Secretary of State Sumner Welles on July 1. Casey frankly and candidly explained the circumstances leading to the adoption of the diversion program, and admitted that it was the requirements of his own Department, the Treasury, which when laid before the cabinet resulted in the decision to adopt the diversion policy. He then took up the U.S.-U.K. talks, confirming the fact that Chamberlain had made an earnest plea for the cooperation of the Dominions in reconsidering their preference agreements. Casey expressed confidence that Australia would make the necessary adjustments, *but* the Australian government wanted to know *first* what trade concessions the United States would be able to make to Australia. Here was the rub. Welles proceeded to let Casey know that the United States had no intention of bargaining until the diversion policy was ended and a satisfactory basis for a U.S.-U.K. trade treaty was laid. Welles then went on to pin down Casey on what would be done after the Australian elections, and he exacted from Casey an expression of belief that Australia would make the necessary concessions once the elections were over.[8]

Casey's visit was a success from the American point of view. It gave the officials at the Department a much needed opportunity to clarify the position of the United States and also to gain some insight into the Australian plans for the future. Personally for Casey the visit was a success, too, since he made a good impression upon the men with whom he dealt. "The crowd across the water," the Department learned from the London embassy, "think Casey the smartest of the lot—future P.M., etc."[9] In terms of Australian objectives, however, Casey's talks could hardly be termed a victory. The Lyons ministry was hoping desperately to receive some hint from the United States on concessions to Australia, but Casey achieved nothing in this direction. "Casey tried very hard," Minter noted in a letter to his colleague in the Division of Western European Affairs John Hickerson, "to focus attention upon a United States-Australia agreement. He got nothing out of us, either general or particular."[10]

In the succeeding months Washington stuck to its position while the Lyons ministry sought a face-saving formula. Perhaps Washington could not have done otherwise, for there was a deeper logic in the American position than lack of sympathy for Lyons or irritation over the discriminations of the diversion program. The United States was bargaining with London for concessions in the United Kingdom market, and to obtain them it had to give concessions to the United Kingdom in the American market. If these were evenly balanced, and then, in addition, the United States had to make concessions to the Dominions for what it was receiving in the United Kingdom market, the United States would be paying in two directions at once. Moffat, in a letter to Trade Commissioner Squire at Sydney, set forth the Department's reasoning:

> We made it plain that if payment were demanded by the Dominions before agreeing to a modification of the preferences, such payment must be made by Great Britain and not by the United States. Britain, for instance, could agree to give up certain of her preferences in the Dominions market which would be a *quid pro quo* in that it would enable the Dominions to negotiate further trade agreements.
>
> While not rejecting this point of view the British to date have offered the Dominions very little in the way of return payment for a modification of their preference; in fact, I feel that she has encouraged the Dominions to continue to demand direct compensation from the United States and should there be simultaneous negotiation between the United States and the Dominions, we would risk being maneuvered into a position of paying twice.[11]

These considerations made the Department reluctant to undertake simultaneous negotiations with the Dominions. The United States did undertake parallel negotiations with Canada, but the Australian diversion program and the risks of "paying twice" were to prevent negotiating concurrently with Australia.

The first problem to be worked out, however, was how to end the discriminations of the diversion program, and since this could not be done until after the Australian elections, the trade issue marked time for some months. Officials at the Department of State awaited anxiously the Australian October elections, hoping that promptly thereafter action would be taken to end the diversion program. Indications that further delay would ensue brought a sharp response from the Department. When a report reached Washington in September that the Australian Assistant Secretary of the Department of Trade and Customs, Arthur C. Moore, had stated that there would be no change in the trade policy and that prospects for a trade agreement were "very bright," Moffat summoned Officer for a straight-from-the-shoulder talk. Moffat, now chief of the newly reorganized Division of European Affairs, told Officer that if Moore indicated that the Australian diversion policy was hastening a trade agreement he was "talking through his hat." An even greater reaction took place when Officer stated that the diversion policy might not be altered until February or March of 1938 because it would be "unpopular to do anything immediately." Moffat informed him that the United States had more or less committed itself to do nothing until the elections were passed, but its patience was running "extremely thin" and the government might feel very differently about it if further delay ensued.[12]

By early October Officer was more optimistic that action was imminent. The Australian Parliament, not having passed the budget, would meet again in November, and considerable work had been done on the tariff measures which must be devised to replace the licensing system.[13] Then came the elections, and Lyons' United Australia party won a victory at the polls. Within a short time thereafter rumors circulated in Sydney commercial circles that the diversion policy would be dropped when Parliament met for a short session beginning November 30.[14] Just before Parliament assembled Consul Doyle reported indications that a favorable atmosphere was being created for a change of policy. "During the past three weeks or so there has been a great campaign here in the press urging closer relations with the U.S.—with particular emphasis on the idea of closer political collaboration." Doyle also reported that the Sydney *Morning Herald* and other Sydney newspapers were advocating dropping of the trade diversion policy.[15]

On December 7 the Lyons government suddenly took action. The Minister for Trade and Customs, Thomas W. White, announced to the House on the afternoon of that day sweeping changes in the licensing system. He explained that the government planned to end the licensing system and substitute a system of adequate duties where necessary to protect Australian industry. This would be accomplished early in 1938 when the Parliament met for its regular session. Until that time the licensing system would be administered as follows: 1) licenses would be granted irrespective of country of origin for goods not competitive with Australian industry; 2) licenses for goods competitive with Australian industry would be issued as in the past until adequate duties could be applied; and 3) importation of motor chassis would continue under the quota.[16] The Ministry's decision to end the diversion system had come with great suddenness. On the morning of the day White made his announcement, his chief adviser Arthur C. Moore was closeted with the new American consul general, Thomas M. Wilson, telling him that the United States must give indications of concessions before the diversion program would be withdrawn. Wilson was quite surprised upon attending the meeting of the House that afternoon to hear White's announcement. He later learned from Moore and others that the decision had been made that same morning at a meeting of the cabinet.[17] The cabinet meeting apparently had been stormy. Officer later told Moffat that there had been "the devil of a row" in the cabinet and the change had been approved by a very small majority.[18]

Washington was elated at the announcement of the immediate modification and eventual elimination of the licensing system. The next weeks were crowded, however, with conferences and communications across the Pacific as the Department sought to determine whether all the discrimination actually had been eliminated. Australia pressed for an immediate restoration of the benefits accruing under the reciprocal trade program and the opening of trade talks, but Hull and others were by no means certain that Australia could as yet qualify for "de-blacklisting," as the Australians called it. Officer insisted at the Department that in the interim until the licensing system ended, there would be no discrimination. He had to concede, however, that the phraseology in White's announcement was ambiguous and that the change was being accomplished by a timid government in such a way as to avoid a reaction in the country.[19]

As more information arrived at the Department, particularly from Consul General Wilson at Sydney, it became increasingly apparent that all discriminations had indeed not ended. Wilson reported much confusion in Australian government circles. Some members of the cabinet thought the intention of the government was to end all discrimination, as Attorney General Menzies insisted. Lieutenant Colonel Hodgson, Secretary at the Ministry for External Affairs, agreed with Wilson, however, that "after all discrimination had not entirely disappeared in fact." The Ministry, Wilson reported, was doing some face-saving and was "terribly embarrassed by prior commitments given to Australian manufacturers, who may be in a position to cause political death to those who now seek to go back upon those commitments."[20] As Wilson studied the changing program, he concluded that the discriminations had not ended. Of the eighty-five items originally on the licensing list, twenty-one remained under restriction in late December.[21] On those items still under regulation the Australian government had supplied no assurance that licenses would be granted on a nondiscriminatory basis.

In an attempt to clear up the prevailing uncertainty, Wilson had a long talk with Lyons, which he reported to the Department on December 23. Despite what Officer and British Ambassador Lindsay had said about discrimination being at an end, Lyons said that the Australian government was not claiming that "all discrimination" had ceased but rather that "substantial discrimination" had ceased. On the basis of this, Australia expected the United States to enter informal discussions immediately on a trade treaty. Lyons gave assurances at the same time that the entire licensing system would be abolished soon, but he added that commitments given to Australian industries, together with political risks, prevented him from doing more than had been done. If the United States demanded more and required Australia to "toe the line," he must refuse. Wilson, after listening to Lyons, was convinced that Washington should not make Australia "toe the line." He urged the Department to accept the Australian position and proceed with the "deblacklisting" and trade talks. "The Department's decision will be made of course in the fuller light of facts unknown to me," wrote Wilson, "but I cannot help feeling that if we now stand upon strict observance of the letter rather than the principle of our policy of refusing to negotiate as long as any form of discrimination exists, both the Government and the public will be convinced that their good faith has been questioned resulting in a sense of humiliation and hurt and the swing of the pendulum away from the United States will be far and very slow in returning."[22]

A further period of confusion transpired at Washington before officials realized just how far principle would have to be stretched. Wilson's telegraphed report of his talk with Lyons should have made it plain to the Department that the Australian government was unwilling to commit itself on issuing licenses without discrimination on the items still remaining under the system. The Australian liaison officer and the British ambassador, however, were poorly informed on the Australian position and the Department assumed from their remarks that the ending of "substantial discrimination" meant that licenses would be issued on a nondiscriminatory basis. All officials of the Department concerned attended a conference in Assistant Secretary of State Francis B. Sayre's office and agreed unanimously to remove Australia from the blacklist and to begin exploratory conversations regarding a trade agreement. It was estimated that the items still on the restricted list constituted only three per cent of America's export trade to Australia, and it was assumed that on those there would be a fair allocation of licenses.[23] The Department then prepared to take Australia off the blacklist. While doing so, Hull cabled Wilson to get assurances from Lyons that licenses would be awarded without discrimination on the items still regulated.[24] This was doubtless done largely for the record, for the Department seemed confident that the assurances would be readily forthcoming.

Within a few days Washington learned, much to its dismay, that Lyons was not willing to supply the desired assurances. Officer came to the Department on January 14, 1938, with a telegram from Canberra containing the news. Officer said gloomily that he had thought his government would give the desired assurances, and he was frankly concerned at the trend things were taking. Could not some formula be found to circumvent the impasse, he inquired? Could not the United States commence informal trade talks at once, before the "de-blacklisting" had been completed? To this last question Moffat gave a definite no.[25] News from Sydney soon supplemented Officer's information. Wilson reported that Lyons was "put out at being expected to give further assurances and felt a loss of dignity of his position as head of the State because of the demand." The Prime Minister told Wilson bluntly that he could give no unqualified assurance of the nature asked by the Department. Despite this Wilson continued to urge upon Washington a realistic view:

> I am not sympathetic towards the position in which the Australian Government now finds itself; furthermore the viciousness of their discriminatory policy in the past strikes me with greater force as I delve into it. But I do counsel a realistic view of the present situation providing of course that we wish to enter into discussions with them at all. Assurances already received are not without weight; expressions of future intentions are sincere. Any course taken by us which lacks realism will create bad feeling at a time when good feeling should be cultivated.[26]

The Department was in a perplexing position. As Assistant Secretary Sayre pointed out to British Ambassador Lindsay, a crucial matter of principle affecting the whole trade agreement program was at stake. When the reciprocal trade act was being passed back in 1934, opposition Congressmen charged that the only result of the act would be that foreign nations would immediately raise their tariff rates or initiate discriminatory measures against the United States in order to improve their bargaining position and obtain concessions for either reducing padded rates or removing discriminations. The Department had at that time taken the stand that it would not negotiate under these circumstances and had in subsequent years adhered to that principle. Moreover, other countries, including Germany, were now pressing the United States to start discussions while discriminations remained. If the principle were yielded in the case of Australia, the United States would be in an untenable position with those countries.[27]

Lyons, in attempting to maneuver himself out of an embarrassing spot, had now maneuvered Washington into a difficult position. The ministry had ended most of the licensing system, announced that it would end completely in March, but had stated categorically that some discrimination would continue until that time. Concurrently Lyons made it clear to the American government that he expected "de-blacklisting" and trade talks to take place immediately. Washington was now torn between the desire to uphold a principle and the wish to prevent further ill-will between the countries. Though not eager, Washington was at least ready for trade talks. By 1938 the agricultural conditions in the United States had measurably improved,[28] and furthermore the Department, in order to facilitate the U.S.-U.K. negotiations, had made it generally known that talks with the Dominions would naturally follow the negotiations with the home government. No doubt some officials at Canberra thought that the diversion policy brought the United States to agree to trade talks, but this factor probably had little if any influence on Washington's willingness to open informal discussions. The American government was very interested, however, in the success of the U.S.-U.K. treaty project, and it was felt that the formal negotiations with the United Kingdom would be furthered if informal talks were carried on with Australia. Then, if the conversations gave promise of success, formal negotiations could be undertaken after the conclusion of the U.S.-U.K. treaty. But now Canberra, desirous of trade talks for many years, was making it painfully difficult for the United States to begin them.

The American government was earnestly endeavoring to break the impasse. Assistant Secretary Sayre abandoned one position after another. Until this time the Department had absolutely refused to commit itself to trade talks following the "de-blacklisting," even though the decision had been made to undertake them. Now Sayre told Officer that the United States would consent to proceed with informal confidential discussions to see whether a basis for a trade agreement existed. This would follow immediately after the "de-blacklisting." Sayre also relinquished the demand for assurance of nondiscriminatory treatment during the interval before the licensing system came to an end. He now suggested a formula stating only that licenses would be "liberally" issued.[29]

The deadlock was broken on January 22. Officer brought a telegram from Lyons which, though it contained no specific assurances even under the revised formula, satisfied the Department. Lyons in this message spread all his cards on the table, detailing the reasons for the Australian position. Licenses were being issued freely for all but fifteen items, he explained. Four of the fifteen were subject to quotas of which the United States had the largest share. On many of the eleven remaining items licenses were being issued, though the government had not found it possible to announce it. Any discrimination that remained was confined to a few items, the total value of which from all countries was estimated to be less than £200,000 in a full year, or £25,000 during the remaining six weeks of the licensing system. Lyons frankly admitted that discrimination on this small group of items could not be immediately ended because the government had either undertaken to issue licenses for imports from certain foreign countries or, in the interests of Australian manufacturers, had agreed not to permit the import of these goods from the United States. Lyons expressed the hope that in view of these facts the United States would appreciate that the licensing system would affect such a negligible proportion of American trade that it would consider that "substantial discrimination" no longer existed.[30]

The Department was now ready to stretch principle far enough to cover the admitted but relatively minor discrimination that remained. The Division of European Affairs, including Moffat, Minter, and Hickerson, agreed that the Department should go forward with the "de-blacklisting" at once.[31] Just three days after Officer brought Lyons' message to the Department, Hull cabled Wilson that the President had ordered that beginning February 1, 1938, the products of Australia be accorded most-favored-nation tariff treatment.[32]

Thus the acrimonious trade dispute which had lasted for more than a year and a half was closed. In summing up, it is difficult to name any significant favorable results from the diversion program. Perhaps Australian manufacturers and British commercial interests obtained some short-term benefits, but those advantages hardly compensated for the damage Australia suffered politically. Japan, from whence came Australia's major threat of aggression, took great offense at the Australian policy and found in that policy (along with similar policies of other countries to exclude Japanese products) justification for her expansionist program. The United States, though reacting less vigorously, would not soon forget the discrimination. The diversion program had accentuated the unfavorable impression created in Washington by the proposal of June 4, 1934. As the program was concluded, many in Australia discerned that it had been a failure. Senator Gordon Brown doubtless expressed the feeling of a large number of Australians when he stood upon the floor of Parliament and evaluated the program in a few short sentences: "Honestly I do not think our trade diversion policy worried America more than a fly does a horse, or a flea a dog. . . . A relatively small country like this cannot have upon America or the British Empire or the rest of the world the effect that some people here imagine."[33] The comment of Sir Frederick Eggleston was equally apt. What the trade diversion program achieved, he observed, was "a maximum of irritation with a minimum of benefit."[34]

It was, of course, Britain's compelling necessity for a rapprochement with the United States that ended trade diversion. The projected U.S.-U.K. trade treaty was far more important politically than commercially, and Australia had no choice but to cooperate. The meaning of the Anglo-American trade negotiations was plain to all concerned. Chamberlain wrote in 1937: "The reason why I have been prepared to go a long way to get this treaty, is precisely because I reckoned it would help to educate American opinion to act more and more with us, and because I felt sure it would frighten the totalitarians."[35] Australians also discerned the importance of the trade treaty. In a collection of articles published in 1938 under the title *Australia's Foreign Policy,* distinguished Australian writers frequently referred to the great political importance of the Anglo-American trade negotiations and the necessity of Australian cooperation.[36] Thus in matters of trade, as in the Matson dispute, the influence of the mother country was the determining factor governing United States-Australian relations.

CHAPTER FIVE

Trade Talks, 1938-1939

THE exploratory talks for a trade agreement which began in Washington in February, 1938, were launched in an atmosphere that gave little promise of success. The legacy of the past few years represented a heavy liability. When Moffat, Sayre, and Harry C. Hawkins discussed the Australian situation with Hull in January, they found him "bitterly resentful of Australian perverseness during the past two years."[1] Moffat wrote to Consul General Wilson in the same month saying that though there was a wish on the part of a number of officials in the Department to "let by-gones be by-gones," there was still "a large undercurrent of resentment at what Australia has done." Moffat felt that Australian officials did not fully realize this. "I do not think," he told Wilson, "that the Australians ever quite appreciated the fact that because we did not have tantrums we did not really care."[2]

During the trade war Australia had created a further source of irritation by adopting intermediate tariff rates. Since 1932 Washington had been much annoyed by the empire preferential system, and then in 1936 Australia adopted the practice of granting tariff rates intermediate between the preferential rates and the general rates. During 1936 and 1937 Australia conceded intermediate rates on many items to Belgium, Czechoslovakia, and France; and many other countries enjoyed intermediate rates by virtue of most-favored-nation status. By early 1938 of fifty-seven countries trading with Australia, thirty-four enjoyed most-favored-nation treatment and intermediate rates. Of the twenty-three others, all had little trade with Australia except the United States, Japan, Greece, Turkey, and Switzerland.[3] When the intermediate rates were accorded

49

to other countries but not the United States, the Department of State made no protest but only because it was preoccupied with the more onerous discriminations of the diversion regulations. Moffat told Wilson in January, 1938, that he should not let the Australians think that, because no protest was made, the United States accepted the situation. "At the time," he explained to Wilson, "we were not discussing matters with the Australians, and, more than that, the only retaliatory action we could have taken was to black-list them, which had already been done."[4]

In addition to the ill-will generated by the trade diversion program and the intermediate tariff rates, an even more difficult hurdle remained for the trade talks to surmount. Congressional elections in the United States would be held in November, 1938, and the Roosevelt administration had to consider the political risks of making concessions to Australian agricultural products, particularly wool. In January, Secretary of Agriculture Henry A. Wallace actually vetoed any possibility of dealing with wool before the November elections,[5] and apparently only reluctantly did he agree later in the month that the trade talks might begin. Moffat pointed out the political obstacles when he wrote to Wilson in January:

> As to negotiations, that represents a more difficult matter and is tied up with all sorts of political considerations. The Australians waited the better part of a year to get through their elections, and by doing so approach us just about the time we have to take our electoral considerations into account.

Moffat indicated, nevertheless, that despite the political risks the Department was ready to tackle the issue. "However," he confided to Wilson, "we shall see what we can do, and there is a predisposition to be as helpful as possible in the circumstances."[6]

Just as the trade talks were getting underway in Washington, an event helped to create a friendlier atmosphere in United States–Australian relations: the visit of American cruisers to Australia. Sydney was at this time celebrating its sesquicentennial, and the United States, along with other powers, was invited to send warships to the celebration. While plans were being drafted for the Sydney visit, the United Kingdom requested that an American squadron also come to Singapore for the formal opening of new docks there.[7] As the United States ships were the only foreign vessels invited to Singapore, this call would have obvious political connotations. The State Department, deciding that both visits would be beneficial politically, arranged for the cruisers *Trenton, Memphis, Milwaukee,* and *Louisville* to visit Sydney. After three days there the first three ships would proceed to Singapore while the *Louisville* remained in Sydney a longer time and then stopped at Melbourne, Hobart, and Adelaide.[8]

The visits took place on schedule and were very successful. On the day the *Louisville* was to depart from Sydney, however, a tragic harbor accident occurred when an Australian passenger craft capsized near the *Louisville* with a loss of nineteen persons. The American naval personnel received high praise from the Sydney press for their part in the rescue of about one hundred and fifty passengers. Seven of the officers and men who had dived from the high decks of the cruiser to save Australian lives were later awarded silver medals for their gallantry by the Royal Shipwreck Relief and Humane Society of New South Wales.[9]

In Washington in the meantime the difficult trade talks had gotten underway. Early in February, Keith Officer, the Australian "liaison officer," had begun conversations with Assistant Secretary of State Sayre and the members of the Division of Trade Agreements. From the outset the participants had to cope with two problems: 1) to determine whether a basis existed for formal trade negotiations, and 2) to decide upon a suitable time for those formal negotiations if a satisfactory basis were found to exist. In other words, they had to decide—as Officer put it—the "whether" and the "when."

Achieving a suitable basis for negotiations at this stage presented no great obstacle. The two sides exchanged tentative lists of concessions, and by early March the participants agreed that these lists would provide a basis for negotiations.[10] There had been, however, no meeting of minds. Both the American and Australian lists of requests were so vague that Sayre and Officer did not really come to grips with the question of a basis for negotiations. The Australian list, for instance, merely requested a reduction on wool rates without indicating how substantial a reduction might be required.[11] The lack of precision in the early talks later necessitated reconsideration of the basis for negotiations, but at this point Sayre and Officer passed on to the matter of the timing of the formal discussions.

The timing proved to be a difficult problem. The Australian government was eager to launch the negotiations and to conclude the definitive agreement speedily. At the outset of the conversations, however, Officer had been apprised that the announcement of negotiations of such controversial character before the November congressional elections might pose serious difficulties.[12] By March 11 the Department was so concerned about the political difficulties that Officer and Ambassador Lindsay were told that the setting of a time for negotiations would have to be postponed indefinitely. Sayre explained that he had talked with Hull, and it had been decided that the political risks were too great, that it would be best to mark time to see how the situation developed. Because of the negotiations with Britain the Eastern states had already attacked the reciprocal trade program, and if the woolgrowing Western states were drawn into the opposition through negotiations with Australia, it might defeat the entire program. This was a risk, Sayre pointed out, which Australia and the United Kingdom shared with the Roosevelt administration.[13]

Unquestionably, the Department was sincere in its desire to negotiate a trade agreement with Australia and the political risks were indeed very real. Hull had made soundings on Capitol Hill and found no willingness to support any treaty that would involve a reduction in the duty on raw wool.[14] The Australian government, nevertheless, was bitterly disappointed at the delay. Officer protested that the Australian Parliament would soon meet and the ministry would be seriously embarrassed if an announcement of negotiations could not be made.[15] Ambassador Lindsay likewise told Sayre that the Australian government also had a thorny political problem which would become more difficult if the United States refused to proceed with the negotiations.[16]

Despite Lindsay's sympathy for the Australian plight, Sayre succeeded in enlisting his aid in placating the Australian government. In a private conference with Lindsay, Sayre pointed out that the United States-United Kingdom agreement constituted the "disideratum of paramount importance," and that Britain should assist in making the Australian government comprehend the risks to the Anglo-American treaty if the formal negotiations with Australia were undertaken. Lindsay acknowledged that he quite understood these considerations and was confident that his government would aid in appeasing the Australians. He observed, however, that the American government probably overrated the ability of the British government to do this. But, said Lindsay, the United Kingdom agreement "is the trunk" and the Australian agreement "is only a branch," and "while the branch is important, we must not jeopardize the trunk for the sake of it."[17]

The following month some of the members of the Australian delegation to London passed through Washington, including Edwin Abbott, Comptroller General of Customs, and J. Frank Murphy, Secretary of the Department of Commerce. When they urged that the United States take up negotiations with Australia along with Canada and the United Kingdom so that the whole question of preference in relation to American trade might be dealt with simultaneously, Sayre offered little encouragement. Abbott confided that the government had rushed through its plans to abandon the licensing system in the hope of obtaining a place in the scheme, and heavy disappointment would result if Australia could not be included. Lacking some definite word on negotiations from the United States, Abbott hinted, the delegation at London might find it difficult to go through with the tentative concessions to which Australia had consented to facilitate the U.S.-U.K. agreement.[18]

Washington marked time for only six weeks. In May the Australian government ended the licensing system on all items except motor cars, and State Department officials were favorably impressed. By early June prime consideration was being attached to the question of proceeding with the treaty project. After conferring with Roosevelt, Hull, and Secretary of Agriculture Wallace, Sayre met with Department officials on June 4. Wallace, Sayre reported, was not fully convinced that negotiations should be attempted before the November elections, but if they were undertaken, the emphatic deadline for completion must be September 10. Roosevelt, Sayre said, thought the treaty project "probably" should be tackled but the agreement should be signed by September 1. Sayre believed that Hull was still opposed to undertaking the project before the elections, but the assembled officials recommended unanimously that the Department proceed immediately with the negotiations. All agreed that American commerce with Australia might suffer greatly by failure to do so. Moreover, it was obvious that Australian cooperation in facilitating the U.S.-U.K. agreement would be more readily forthcoming if negotiations were launched.[19] A week later, at a White House conference Roosevelt, Wallace, and Sayre agreed to crowd the Australian agreement through by September 15.[20]

On June 13 the Department notified the British embassy that it was prepared to go forward immediately with the treaty project if certain conditions could be met. The treaty must be signed by early September or an announcement must be made that the negotiations had been terminated. In order to complete the procedural requirements for public notice and hearings under the Trade Agreements Act, the commencement of negotiations must therefore be announced not later than July 7. Since the time available was very limited and since preferably no public announcement should be made unless it was clear that the project could be successfully completed, the Department now reopened the entire question of whether a basis for agreement existed. July 7 was stipulated as the deadline for determining by a more precise indication of possible concessions whether the negotiations could succeed. The Department also stated that the conclusion of the U.S.-U.K. trade agreement was a necessary prerequisite to the conclusion of the treaty with Australia.[21]

The Australian and American governments now focused on precise concessions and requests. On the crucial item of wool the United States stated that it could not consider lowering the tariff below twenty-five cents per pound of clean content and twenty-eight cents on scoured wool. This represented a reduction of about twenty-six and one-half per cent of the existing duties. The United States also offered to bind duties on frozen beef, veal, and mutton and to lower duties on many other minor items of interest to Australia. In return the United States asked for reduction in Australian tariffs as follows: automobile chassis reduced to parity with Canada with no quota restrictions; twenty per cent reduction in duties on automobile parts; no preference on automobile engines; and reductions on a long list of items, including appliances, machinery, tools, and typewriters.[22]

The Department realized that the offer was not the sweeping revision Australia desired, but considered that no more could be risked in the political situation then existing. Moffat's diary entry for June 13, the day the American requests were presented, illustrates this:

> The British Ambassador came in at our request to talk over the Australian situation. We explained that we had always said that if it were politically possible we would go ahead and negotiate with Australia, but we could not inject wool into an election. However, circumstances were such that we were able to put up a certain proposition on a "take it or leave it" basis. We wanted to make it clear that this was not an ultimatum, and whether or not it was accepted our feelings would be just the same. It was, however, an offer limited in scope, to do something at the moment, and if the idea commended itself to the Australian authorities we could then go into further details.[23]

Soon it became apparent that the Australians regarded the proposals as falling far short of what they desired. Officer lunched with Moffat on June 23 and told him frankly that the proposals had not been well received by the Australian delegation in London. Sir Earle Page, the Deputy Prime Minister and Minister for Commerce, was annoyed at the "take it or leave it" nature of the proposals presented under a deadline. He regarded the wool concession as less than what Australia considered the minimum and was indignant at the offer to bind meat at its present prohibitive rate. None of the requests were impossible of consideration, Officer assured Moffat, but the Australians thought the United States was asking a great deal more than she was willing to give.[24]

When the Australian reply came, it indicated that the two countries were poles apart on their conceptions of a trade agreement. An Australian list of concessions and requests was presented on June 28 which offered only to bind intermediate tariff rates. In return Australia requested a rate of twenty-two cents on wool. The Australian government's observations on the American proposal indicated that a fundamental difference divided the two governments in their approach to a trade treaty. While the United States anticipated an agreement with concessions balanced approximately equally, the Australian government conceived of a convention which would redress the extremely unfavorable balance of trade. "To be of value to Australia," the Australian communication said, "an agreement must promise a more even balance in trade between the two countries and contain concessions which will make possible some expansion of the Australian export trade to the United States of America, for the Commonwealth Government cannot contemplate a continuance indefinitely of anything approaching the figure of the present annual adverse balance." The Australian government asserted that the American proposals, if adopted, would likely increase Australia's adverse balance of trade.[25]

The Department immediately dispatched a note to Lindsay stating that the essentials of a trade agreement could not be agreed upon before July 7.[26] For a week, however, the Department tried to save the talks from failure. On July 6 Sayre and his associates held a critical conference with Secretary of Agriculture Wallace. They concluded that if any progress were to be made with Australia, the wool tariff must be set below the twenty-five-cent level previously authorized by Wallace and Roosevelt. Australia had made it clear that she would not consider anything above twenty-two cents, and Sayre now pressed Wallace to sanction the lower figure. Wallace agreed that the proposal to set it at twenty-two cents was economically sound. "However," said Wallace, "we frankly have to face the fact that the question before us is a political rather than an economic one." The political considerations, to Wallace's mind, predominated. He therefore refused to agree to the lower figure. He suggested that Sayre go to the White House and secure consent for the reduction, but Sayre said he was not willing to do this.[27] Later, the same day this conference was held, Hickerson and Hawkins told Officer that it would be impossible to reach a decision on the wool tariff question in the time available and that the project for a treaty must be abandoned at least until after the congressional elections.[28]

The collapse of the treaty project at this time was not due to American political conditions alone. The Department of State was naturally reluctant to go forward with the project over the opposition of the Department of Agriculture, but evidence suggests that Hull and his associates were willing to assume the political risks alone if Australia offered a reasonable *quid pro quo* for the twenty-two-cent rate on wool. Before the project went up in smoke on July 6, Officer was pressed for a definite indication of what Australia would give in return, and all that Officer could offer, after contacting London, was the binding to the United States of present intermediate rates. Department of State officials were literally amazed that Australia offered so little in return for the wool reduction, and they were unwilling to undertake the political risks under those circumstances.[29] Indeed, the officials at the Department were so appalled at the Australian proposal that they would probably have been ready to drop the trade talks even if no political considerations had been present.

The trade talks were not to be resumed until the Roosevelt administration had passed the pitfalls, real and imaginary, of the November congressional elections. In the interim, the Department was permitted an insight into the feelings of Sir Earle Page, who had been in London negotiating the renewal of the Ottawa agreement. Page passed through the United States on his way home from London in August, and while in Washington he unburdened himself freely to Department officials. When Moffat stressed that Australian leaders should say nothing in Australia to complicate the administration's political difficulties before the congressional elections, Page retorted that if American officials thought the Australian government could remain silent until November they did not know the Australian public. The Australian people, he exclaimed, knew that Australia had made definite sacrifices in order to bring about a U.K.-U.S. trade agreement, that Canada had done the same, that Canada had been rewarded with new negotiations and Australia had been "shut out in the cold." He added further that if the American proposals for an agreement of six weeks before were made public, it would so anger the Australian people that negotiations would be out of the question for twenty years! If the United States continued snubbing Australia, he said, the ministry would have to bring down new tariff measures designed to divert American trade.[30]

The Department did not believe Page's indignation typified the feelings of most Australian leaders, but his remarks nevertheless had a definite effect. Throughout 1938 Hull had evidenced some reluctance to go forward with the talks because he still resented the treatment Australia had accorded American trade during 1936-1937. "What you may not realize," Moffat wrote to Consul General Wilson, "is quite how deeply disturbed the Secretary was per-

sonally by the trade diversion program which he has never for-
given nor forgotten." Moffat confided to Wilson, however, that
when Hull read a memorandum containing Page's remarks, he was
profoundly impressed. "In fact, between ourselves," wrote Moffat,
"I think it did more to convince the Secretary that despite opposition from Agriculture we must as a self-protective measure go ahead
and negotiate with Australia after elections than any other one document that has been put before his eyes."[31]

On November 15, the elections safely over, Hull made the anticipated new approach to Australia, suggesting that they begin
again with the question of whether a basis for an agreement existed. The Lyons ministry could now turn more leisurely to consideration of a trade treaty, for it had safely weathered the announcement of the U.S.-U.K. treaty in early November. Australia
had granted concessions in the United Kingdom market to facilitate this treaty, such as agreeing to the abolition of the duty on
fresh apples during August 15-April 15 and fresh pears during
August through January, and reductions in duties on honey and
preserved fruits.[32] Despite the fact that these concessions were accorded without receiving any American concessions to balance
them, the public reaction which the ministry had feared did not
materialize.[33]

When it arrived in December, 1938, the Australian reply to
Hull's initiative indicated that the two governments were still far
apart on their conceptions of a trade agreement. The note clearly
revealed that Australia was not interested in a treaty giving equivalent concessions. Such an agreement would merely perpetuate a
situation which Australia regarded as insufferable. The treaty must
substantially redress Australia's unfavorable balance of trade with
the United States.[34] Officials at the Department of State had little
sympathy for this conception of the proposed treaty. At Washington the American tariffs were regarded as no more extraordinarily
high than those affecting American imports into Australia. Officials
believed that American goods had won a large part of the Australian market in spite of notoriously high tariffs and large margins of
imperial preference. The disparity in the trade was therefore due
not to high tariff rates on one side alone, but rather to the fact that
in the context of high tariff rates on both sides, the force of con-

sumer demand weighed heavily in favor of the United States. There was great demand in Australia for American goods, whereas in the United States there was a great surplus of many of the items that Australia exported. Officials at the Department made it clear to Officer when he delivered the Australian note that the United States would not accept the Australian position. Harry C. Hawkins, Chief of the Division of Commercial Treaties and Agreements, told Officer bluntly that the United States considered the whole question of bilateral trade balances irrelevant and would not negotiate on the basis of attempting bilateral balancing.[35] Thus as the trade talks resumed the prospects for success were as dim as ever.

The Australian note asked that the United States facilitate the progress of the talks by indicating the "maximum" concessions which it would make on wool, mutton, lamb, beef, and butter. Although the Department regarded this as an extraordinary request, it undertook to comply. The crucial item was wool, and Officer had stated to Department officials that he believed this item alone was considered a *sine qua non* in Australia. The question of wool was therefore raised again with the Department of Agriculture. Sayre called on Wallace as he had the previous July and attempted to enlist his support for a twenty-two-cent duty. The November elections had apparently not bolstered Wallace's confidence. He told Sayre that the political repercussions would be "very serious," and on that ground he refused to endorse the twenty-two-cent rate. Wallace nevertheless did not veto the lower rate; he merely refused to accept any of the responsibility for such a move. He pointed out to Sayre that a recent Gallup poll showed eighty-five per cent of the Americans polled to be in favor of Hull's trade policy, and with that strength the Department of State should be able to carry the wool reduction without the assistance of the Department of Agriculture.[36]

The November elections obviously had not ended the Roosevelt administration's concern over the political aspects of an Australian treaty. Moffat noted in his diary on December 17 that "the Trade Agreement Division and Sayre are frightfully worried over the political opposition in the Senate to the Trade Agreement program."[37] That anxiety heightened in January, 1939, when Senator Joseph C. O'Mahoney of Wyoming publicly demanded explicit assurance from the Department of State that wool would be completely eliminated from the treaty conversations with Australia.[38] Despite the political risks, Moffat urged a policy of courage rather than "safety first" as some officials were advocating.[39]

As the United States undertook to draft a list of requests to present to Australia, it became increasingly apparent that the minimum Australian demand on wool would not be met. By January, 1939, Sayre and his associates had concluded that they could not go below twenty-five or twenty-four cents. On January 10 Sayre told Officer that he had seen Wallace and the President, and he had not secured authority to go below twenty-five cents. Officer pleaded against a repetition of this offer. His instructions, he confided, were to press for a fifty per cent reduction, that is, a seventeen-cent rate, though he considered an offer of twenty-two cents by the United States would persuade the Australian government at least to contemplate bridging the gap. If the United States clung to its twenty-five-cent offer, he was certain that discussions would abruptly cease.[40]

Early in February, 1939, the United States outlined to Officer what it could undertake and what it wished to receive in return. On the crucial item of wool the United States offered a twenty-four-cent rate and requested concessions on lumber and automobiles in return.[41] Upon receiving this information the Australian government apparently relinquished hope of concluding an agreement in the foreseeable future. Month after month passed with no word from Canberra.

By late June of 1939 the Australian government was preoccupied with the crucial issues of world affairs. The pressure of world events and the hopelessness of securing an acceptable treaty now caused the Australian government virtually to abandon the project for a treaty. At the end of June Trade Commissioner Lewis R. Macgregor informed the Department that he had received a personal telegram from Canberra stating: "We are not breaking off negotiations although the position is rendered extremely difficult by inadequacy of United States offers on wool and mutton and lamb and by the extent of their requests."[42] The Department had sensed that the talks were coming to an end but held the Australians responsible for the deadlock. Moffat wrote to Consul General Wilson in June:

It is quite clear now that the Australians have no desire to do anything in the matter of lumber or automobiles, which means that the explorations will dry up, and thanks, this time, to Canberra's intransigence. I think there have been times in the past when our position has been wooden but this time they have only themselves to thank.[43]

Thus in June of 1939 the talks came to a fruitless end with each side feeling that the other was at fault. When World War II broke out the following September, the Department had not yet received an official reply from Canberra. The war now interrupted considerations of a treaty.[44]

CHAPTER SIX

The United States and Australia
in World Affairs, 1938-1939

UNITED STATES-Australian relations entered a new and fateful phase during 1938-1939. Matters of far greater concern superseded the old issues of trade and shipping as the world gradually slipped into the abyss of World War II. In the Pacific area tension mounted as the Japanese forces continued their offensive in China, while in Europe the spring of 1938 witnessed the first major development in Nazi expansion as Hitler marched into Austria.

The seizure of Austria in March, 1938, startled Australians and Americans. On March 17, six days after the *Anschluss,* Secretary of State Hull delivered an important speech on foreign policy before the National Press Club in Washington which was widely publicized in the Commonwealth. Hull took up the battle with the isolationists with vigor. "We may seek to withdraw from participation in world affairs," he cautioned his listeners, "but we cannot thereby withdraw from the world itself. Isolation is not a means to security; it is a fruitful source of insecurity."[1] In Australia signs that the United States was moving away from isolationism were hopefully watched, and Hitler's move now made Australians even more aware of their need for American friendship. The *Anschluss,* reported Consul General Wilson, caused astonishment and genuine shock. By no mere coincidence he reported in the same dispatch that propaganda was observable from many sources which sought to encourage closer cooperation between the Empire and the United States and that societies were springing up in various places in Australia to effect this objective.[2]

62

The demise of Austria accelerated the defense programs of both the United States and Australia. In the United States President Roosevelt had asked Congress in January, 1938, for an appropriation of over one billion dollars for naval construction; shortly after Germany's march into Austria the full budget was voted. In Australia the Lyons ministry was then in the second phase of a rearmament program which had been inaugurated in 1933 with a three-year program. Since the inception of the program, appropriations for defense had climbed steadily upward from £3,159,960, in 1932-1933 to £11,500,000 in 1937-1938, and during that time naval strength had been augumented. By 1938 Australia had in commission four cruisers, one flotilla leader, four destroyers, and two escort vessels. The Austrian *coup* now spelled the need for far greater efforts, and when Treasurer Casey brought down the budget for 1938-1939, it contained a defense expenditure of nearly £17,000,000.[3]

The fall of Austria awakened both Americans and Australians to the threat of aggression in Europe, but in the succeeding months United States and Australian policies diverged in attempting to deal with this danger. This was particularly evident during Britain's efforts to come to terms with Italy looking to the recognition of Mussolini's Ethiopian conquest. The British government was interested in establishing a basis for various agreements on African boundaries, but a more important factor was the desire to keep Italy out of the German camp and to ensure peace and security in the Mediterranean.[4] When Washington learned of the Anglo-Italian negotiations, Roosevelt protested to Chamberlain, pointing out the harmful effect these would have upon the whole policy of nonrecognition and particularly the blow that would be dealt America's policy of nonrecognition of Japan's conquests in the Far East. Hull likewise objected to the projected British move. "If any important country like Great Britain," he said to Ambassador Lindsay, "suddenly abandons this principle to the extent of recognizing the Italian conquest of Ethiopia, the desperado nations would capitalize it as a virtual ratification of their policy of outright treaty wrecking and the seizure of land by force of arms."[5]

Throughout the Anglo-Italian negotiations Australia alone of the Dominions displayed positive interest in the development of British policy. In February, 1938, Lyons telegraphed Chamberlain: "We agree that the present situation calls for action, and we feel that the reopening of conversations with Italy is of the utmost importance."[6] Despite the resignation of Eden over the matter and despite opposition criticism in both the United Kingdom and Australia, the Lyons ministry remained loyally behind the Chamberlain policy. In April, 1938, Britain concluded the agreement with Italy, and when it was implemented, Australia accorded *de jure* recognition to Abyssinia's incorporation into the Italian Empire.[7] Though an appeal by Chamberlain finally brought Roosevelt to issue a statement viewing the agreement with "sympathetic interest," the United States never recognized the conquest of Ethiopia.[8]

Though Australians fully backed Britain's efforts toward appeasement in Europe, the policy of appeasement in the Pacific no longer had the strong support in Australia that it once possessed. On the contrary, during 1938 the Lyons ministry experienced great difficulty in preventing waterside workers from applying unofficial sanctions against Japan. Australian workers were willing to institute a policy of sanctions even though the major powers had backed away from any such strong program. The government of Australia was understandably reluctant to allow sanctions to be implemented when neither the United Kingdom nor the United States was willing to do so. Attorney General Menzies, who performed the unpleasant task of breaking the unofficial sanctions on pig iron and other items, earned for himself the nickname "Pig Iron Bob."[9] A renewal of Australian-Japanese friction over trade was avoided only by the conclusion of another stopgap agreement on July 1, 1938.[10]

The policy of appeasement in Europe received its severest test when Germany leveled demands upon Czechoslovakia during May through September of 1938. As the atmosphere of crisis thickened in Europe, Australia viewed the unfolding events with growing concern. Addresses by Hull and Roosevelt in August, 1938, were accorded close attention in Australia. Hull's radio address on August 16 indicated that the administration was taking significant steps away from the traditional path of isolation. Each day's developments, Hull told his listeners, made it more and more clear that America's situation was profoundly affected by happenings elsewhere in the world, and the United States must increasingly struggle, along with other peoples, to support the only program that

could turn the tide of lawlessness and place the world upon the
roadway to peace and security.[11] Two days after Hull's address
Roosevelt delivered his famous Kingston speech in which he gave
assurance that the United States would not stand by idly if domina-
tion of Canadian soil were threatened by another empire.[12] In Australia the President's affirmation to Canada and Hull's address were
warmly praised and carefully analyzed. The Sydney *Morning Herald* commented:

> President Roosevelt's Canadian declaration, following closely upon
> Mr. Cordell Hull's pledge of the United States to an international
> programme of economic and moral reconstruction, marks another
> step of the Administration away from isolation. Both pronounce-
> ments, however, deserve careful scrutiny, for it would be easy, ac-
> cording to predisposition, to make either too much or too little of
> their significance. If they cannot be interpreted as an indication of
> imminent American intervention in world affairs, it would be equally
> rash to dismiss them as empty rhetorical gestures.[13]

When the Czechoslovakian issue reached a peak in September,
1938, both Australia and the United States swung their influence
in the direction of a compromise settlement. The Australian government, though supporting Britain completely, made its views known
at London during the crucial days when peace and war hung in the
balance. Early in the crisis Australia urged the United Kingdom
government to make representations to Czechoslovakia requesting
an immediate public announcement of the most liberal concessions
it could offer. When Chamberlain's conferences with Hitler during
the second and third weeks of September failed to produce a solution, Lyons cabled the Prime Minister counseling a personal appeal to Mussolini to use his influence for peace, and he offered the
services of the Australian Commissioner at London, Stanley M.
Bruce, as an emissary to the Duce.[14] In the meantime, the United
States had also pressed for a compromise settlement. In a personal
message to Chamberlain, Hitler, President Eduard Benes of Czechoslovakia, and Premier Edouard Daladier of France on September
26, President Roosevelt recommended that the negotiations be continued "looking to a peaceful, fair, and constructive settlement of
the questions at issue." The next day Roosevelt sent a second appeal to Hitler; and Roosevelt and Chamberlain both dispatched requests to Mussolini to lend his aid toward a negotiated settlement.
On the twenty-eighth Mussolini dragged Europe from the abyss of

war. Hitler, at the prompting of Mussolini, invited Chamberlain, Daladier, and Mussolini to meet with him at Munich.[15] It is doubtful whether Roosevelt's appeals had a decisive influence in bringing about the Munich settlement, but in Australia the American efforts were applauded.[16] When the agreement was reached, Lyons expressed the appreciation of the Australian people for the great services rendered by Chamberlain, Mussolini, and Roosevelt.[17]

The sense of relief which the Munich accord brought to Australia and the United States was short-lived. Disillusionment soon followed. In December, Consul General Wilson reported that criticism of Chamberlain and his policy of appeasement originated from almost every section of the Australian press.[18] Amid the general disillusionment in the United States, Roosevelt proceeded to take another step away from isolation in his "methods short of war" speech on January 4, 1939. There were, the President told the Congress, "many methods short of war, but stronger and more effective than mere words, of bringing home to aggressor governments the aggregate sentiments of our own people."[19] Australians greeted Roosevelt's message with great satisfaction. "There is a nervousness here," reported Wilson, "because of the isolation of Australia from those quarters whence assistance in an emergency would be expected."[20]

In March, 1939, flagrantly violating the Munich accord, Hitler seized Czechoslovakia. The following month Mussolini invaded Albania. At this juncture Roosevelt decided to appeal directly to Hitler and Mussolini. In a message on April 14 he asked the dictators to give assurances that their armed forces would not attack thirty countries, which were mentioned by name, for a period of ten or twenty-five years, and he offered to secure reciprocal assurances from those countries. Though the request was ridiculed in Berlin and Rome, the democracies acclaimed it enthusiastically. Former Prime Minister William Morris Hughes, then Minister for External Affairs, told the House: "President Roosevelt's message signifies a most timely initiative on the part of the United States. The Commonwealth Government cordially associates itself with the welcome to President Roosevelt's action given by the Government of the United Kingdom." The press in Australia was equally laudatory. ". . . there sits in the White House," said the Melbourne *Herald,* "a lusty, challenging, non-passive liberal who thinks in human and not legalistic terms, and who today is the world's most powerful friend of freedom."[21]

In the same month that President Roosevelt voiced his dramatic appeal, the death of Prime Minister Lyons plunged the Australian government into political dissension. Close associates of Lyons had known for some months that his health was failing, but when he died no provision had been made for a successor. For almost three weeks political confusion reigned before the new Prime Minister was named. When the struggle was over, the victor was Robert G. Menzies, the former Attorney General who had recently resigned from the Lyons cabinet in protest against the tabling of the National Insurance Bill. Menzies had experienced a remarkable rise to political leadership. A Melbourne barrister, he had entered the House of Representatives in 1934 after a brief service in the State Parliament of Victoria. He entered Lyons' cabinet as Attorney General and Minister for Industry in 1934, and by 1935 he had become deputy party leader of the United Australia party. In personality he was Lyons' opposite. Lyons typified the Australian ideal, a plain-spoken "ordinary sort of bloke." Menzies, possessing dignity and poise, labored under the disadvantage of his own brilliance. He suffered the disability of the great advocate in a political world that liked ordinariness. He had the further obstacle of coming to office at the head of a party which was badly divided. Furthermore, the leader of the allied Country Party, Earle Page, who had served as interim Prime Minister after Lyons' death, had been alienated during the political struggle over the succession to Lyons.[22]

Despite the handicaps under which he became Prime Minister, Menzies injected a new energy and perspective into governmental leadership. He named as Minister of Supply and Development Richard G. Casey, a man whom American diplomats had long regarded, along with Menzies, as one of Australia's most capable leaders. In that position Casey would be principally responsible for preparing the Australian economy for war. Menzies also took immediate steps to elevate Australia's status in international and particularly Pacific affairs. In his first broadcast to the nation as Prime Minister on April 26, he stated that in the Pacific, Australia had primary responsibilities and primary risks and that Australia would open new diplomatic contacts in the Pacific area:

Little given as I am to encouraging the exaggerated ideas of Dominion independence and separatism which exists in some minds [he told his listeners], I have become convinced that in the Pacific Australia must regard herself as a principal, providing herself with her own information and maintaining her own diplomatic contacts with foreign powers. I do not mean by this that we are to act in the Pacific as if we were a completely separate power; we must, of course, act as an integral part of the British Empire. We must have the fullest consultation and cooperation with Great Britain, South Africa, New Zealand and Canada. But all these consultations must be on the basis that the primary risk in the Pacific is borne by New Zealand and ourselves. With this in mind, I look forward to the day when we will have a concert of Pacific powers, pacific in both senses of the word. This means increased diplomatic contact between ourselves and the United States, China and Japan, to say nothing of the Netherlands East Indies and the other countries which fringe the Pacific.[23]

In the days following the broadcast it became known that the first Australian legation to be opened abroad would be at Washington.

Moffat, who had been largely responsible for the sending of an Australian liaison officer to Washington in 1937, had also played an instrumental part in Australia's decision to send a minister. In December, 1938, he had urged the project upon High Commissioner Bruce, who was in Washington on a visit. Then Bruce had confided that he had finally concluded that diplomatic relations should be established. Before leaving Washington, Bruce promised Moffat to recommend the project.[24] When Bruce returned to Australia in January, 1939, he urged the step at Canberra, and it was due to his recommendation that the cabinet determined to exchange ministers with the United States. The decision had been made, therefore, before Lyons' death,[25] but not until Menzies' broadcast of April 26 was the first step taken to implement it.

Soon after the broadcast, Menzies informed Consul General Wilson that he would contact London "very soon" and have the proposal for an exchange of ministers presented by the British ambassador. Menzies also confided that Australia might open formal relations with Tokyo, possibly China later on, and eventually the Netherlands East Indies and France.[26] The exchange of ministers between Washington and Canberra was to be delayed for more than six months, however, due to Australia's difficulties in selecting her first minister and the preoccupation of the ministry with the preparations for war.

The decision to send a minister to Washington was the culmination of Australia's efforts in 1939 to further a rapprochement with the United States.With the rising threat to Britain's security, America's friendship could no longer be dismissed as a negligible quantity. The time was gone when the divisive issues of trade and shipping could be allowed to dominate United States-Australian relations. By the time of the Munich agreement both the public and the government of Australia knew this. In December, 1938, Consul General Wilson reported a growing endeavor in Australian editorial comment to understand the American point of view.[27] When the British King and Queen visited the United States in June, 1939, the press in Australia covered it more thoroughly than the visit of the sovereigns to Canada. "There is not a dissentient opinion," reported Wilson, "concerning the importance and success of this visit."[28]

The increasing friendliness toward the United States was due principally to Australia's growing awareness that a friend in the Pacific might be desperately needed in the near future. It was equally true, however, that the Australians could more easily admire the United States as Roosevelt and Hull steered the American public toward a responsible role in international affairs. To be sure, points of friction still remained, but now, late in 1939, the pendulum had at last begun to swing with full force in the direction of friendship.

CHAPTER SEVEN

War in Europe
Brings Appeasement in Asia

THE Menzies ministry, fashioned in a time of tribulation, was soon tempered in the fire of war. From April until late August of 1939, the ministry bent all its energies to the rearmament effort. Then, in the last week of August came the final sequence of events leading to the announcement that Australia was at war. On August 24 the government was informed by London that the German Chancellor had been warned that Britain would honor the guarantee given to Poland following the seizure of Czechoslovakia. In the succeeding days the Australian cabinet held meetings to make the last preparations for entering a state of war. Late in the afternoon of September 1 news of the bombing of Polish cities flashed over the radio, and at 8 P.M. short-wave wireless listeners heard Chamberlain announce that Britain was at war with Germany. At 9:15 P.M. Menzies informed the nation that Great Britain had declared war and that "as a result, Australia is also at war."[1]

Australia's belligerent status immediately raised the issue of American neutrality legislation. Under acts passed during 1935-1937, American citizens were forbidden to sell or transport munitions or armaments to belligerents or to make loans to belligerents. Consul General Wilson visited Canberra on September 8 and found two questions uppermost in the minds of Australian leaders: would the neutrality legislation be repealed, and would the United States help Australia if things got bad? "An atmosphere of bewilderment with touches of grave concern, pessimism and shaken confidence pervades Canberra," Wilson reported.[2]

70

In late September Menzies sent a personal message to Roosevelt urging modification of the neutrality legislation.[3] Roosevelt had already summoned a special session of Congress for that purpose, and when it convened the State Department worked persistently to make the new statute as liberal as possible. In Australia the congressional debate was followed with keen attention. "Faith in Mr. Roosevelt's ability to move mountains and his friendliness towards the Empire is strong," Wilson reported.[4] When in early November legislation was approved permitting belligerents access to war goods on a cash-and-carry basis, Wilson observed profound gratification in Canberra.[5]

In the same month the new neutrality legislation was passed, Australia sent to Washington the first official word of the wish to exchange ministers. In April Menzies had announced the decision to open formal relations, but the ministry's preoccupation with defense and the difficulty of selecting the appointee for the post had delayed implementation of the project. When British Ambassador Lord Lothian presented Australia's official inquiry on exchanging ministers on November 27, Menzies had not yet settled upon an appointee, and Australia suggested that the legation be opened under a chargé d'affaires pending the arrival of a minister in two or three months.[6] By December 15, however, Menzies had decided to send to Washington one of Australia's ablest leaders, Richard G. Casey.[7] Shortly thereafter the United States selected Clarence E. Gauss as its first minister to Australia. At the time of his appointment to Canberra, Gauss held the post of consul general and counselor at Shanghai, and he was regarded as one of the Department's top experts on Far Eastern affairs.

It was some time before the new ministers reached their posts, and in the interim Consul General Wilson had to cope with a new development. In shifting to a wartime economy, Australia adopted on December 1 an import licensing system which applied to all nonsterling countries. Unlike the licensing system of the trade diversion program, these regulations applied without discrimination, and the action was undoubtedly taken to conserve foreign credits for goods needed in warfare. With the memory of the trade diversion program still fresh, however, it was not surprising that American exporters and officials considered the regulations unnecessarily rigorous. As the system worked out in practice, however, the total value of American imports did not decline, though the character of the imports was affected considerably.[8]

Australia and the United States soon faced matters of greater consequence than trade regulations. Casey arrived in Washington in February, 1940, and he was scarcely settled at the new post before Hitler launched his offensives in Europe. The inaction which had characterized the war since the fall of Poland ended suddenly on April 9 when German armies invaded Denmark and Norway. A month later the Wehrmacht moved into the Low Countries. By May 15 the Germans had broken through the French army at Sedan, and the Allies suffered a military disaster of staggering proportions. Britain's new Prime Minister, Sir Winston Churchill, who had taken office on the same day that the Low Countries were invaded, soon faced the task of evacuating British forces from the continent.

As French resistance disintegrated in the first weeks of June, the Allied countries turned desperately to the United States. On June 6 Australian Minister Casey told Hull that he would like the United States to make a declaration of war.[9] In the succeeding days French Premier Paul Reynaud pleaded with the United States to intervene.[10] An American declaration of war was beyond the realm of possibility at this time, but the German advance was so swift that even American intervention could not have saved the Allies from disaster. Roosevelt did, at the request of Prime Minister Menzies, pledge the material resources of the nation,[11] but that promise had more significance for the future than for the present. On the very day that Menzies made the last of two appeals to Roosevelt, Paris fell before the Nazi juggernaut.

The German victories in Europe produced immediate repercussions in the Far East. Both the Netherlands and France had colonies there which were either economically or strategically important to Japan, and the defeat of those nations now provided Japan with a golden opportunity to advance southward. In April Secretary Hull had publicly warned Japan that any alteration of the status quo in the East Indies would endanger the peace of the entire Pacific area. Now with the defeat of the Netherlands in Europe, Hull urged Britain and Australia not to dispatch troops there, for Japan might seize this as an excuse for intervention. On May 10 Assistant Secretary of State Adolf A. Berle, Jr., told Casey that the

United States was not eager to have Allied landings unless definitely at the request of Dutch authorities and under Dutch command.[12] Hull went even further. He told Britain, as he had previously told Japan, that any alteration of the status quo in the Indies would be prejudicial to peace in the entire Pacific area.[13]

In subsequent weeks the Allies followed the American advice and refrained from sending troops, but Australia pressed for firmer American support. On May 16 Casey, on instructions from his government, asked the United States to state publicly that it was not prepared to entertain any attempt at intervention in the Dutch East Indies. Washington was unwilling, however, to go further than general public statements in support of the status quo.[14]

It was soon apparent that Japan's immediate objective was not to invade the Netherlands East Indies but to liquidate the China Incident. On June 17, as the French government sued for an armistice with Germany and Italy, Japan demanded that the French cease shipping materials through French Indochina to China. Within three days France capitulated to the Japanese demands and also agreed to the stationing of Japanese inspectors along the French Indochina railroad to see that the agreement was enforced. France also recognized that Japan had special rights in China to safeguard the security of her army and to maintain order.[15]

The summer of 1940 witnessed a divergence of policy between the United States and the British Commonwealth; in the weeks subsequent to the fall of France, Australia and the United Kingdom tended to follow France down the road of appeasement in the Far East. On June 19 Tokyo demanded that the Burma Road be closed, and London now knew the same kind of pressure that Vichy had experienced. Britain felt that with a German invasion threatening the British Isles she could do little but temporize and, if necessary, appease Japan unless strong American support was forthcoming.

The United States received its first inkling of the new direction of Anglo-Australian policy when on June 26 Casey had a long talk with Stanley K. Hornbeck, the Department's chief adviser on Far Eastern affairs. Casey said that both he and British Ambassador Lothian were advising their governments to come to terms with Japan. He considered it imperative for Britain to enter an agreement with Japan, one that would accord the Japanese what they wanted in China, not "merely a shoestring but something substantial."

Hornbeck told Casey that he could see no virtue in appeasement policies, whether practiced in Europe in 1938 or suggested for trial in East Asia in 1940. He went on to point out what some of the results of appeasement might be, such as: 1) Japan would realize the impotency of the countries and would either decline to make commitments or make them only to break them when she chose, 2) the Japanese military would act more boldly than ever, and 3) Chinese morale would be weakened and Chinese resistance might be ended, thus freeing Japan for adventures to the south. Hornbeck then presented a thesis which Britain was to accept later when the immediate threat of invasion had passed. There was one war going on in the world in two theaters, said Hornbeck, and the Chinese were rendering a valuable service by preventing the Japanese from assisting Germany.[16]

On the following day British Ambassador Lothian presented Hull with an *aide-memoire* which graphically mapped out two courses of action. One was for the United States to tighten pressure on Japan, either by imposing a full embargo on exports to Japan or by sending warships to Singapore, fully cognizant that these steps might result in war. The second course was to negotiate a full settlement with Japan. If the United States could not undertake the first course, then Britain wished to know if the United States would join in making proposals for a Far Eastern settlement.[17] The British proposals were so critical that Hull conferred with Roosevelt before replying. The next day he reviewed the propositions with both Lothian and Casey. As to the first course of action suggested, said Hull, the United States could not send ships to Singapore. On the matter of economic sanctions, he emphasized that the United States had progressively placed more and more restrictions on exports to Japan through moral embargoes and that on several occasions the British government had requested that this policy not be carried too far lest the situation be worsened rather than bettered. As to the second proposal, a Far Eastern settlement, Hull remarked that he had little hope of weaning Japan away from her objectives by offers of intangible concessions or promises of future material assistance. As for tangible concessions, Hull stated a fact that was to become painfully evident in 1941: the United States had nothing tangible in the Far East to offer Japan. Hull said he had no objection if Britain and Australia wished to confer with Japan to see what concessions they could offer, nor would the United States object if they also called upon China and Japan to see what concessions they could make, but, said Hull, no properties or interests of China should be extended to Japan by Britain or by the United States.[18]

Patently, no Far Eastern settlement could be achieved except at the expense of China. The United States had nothing to bargain with in the Far East, and the British and Australians had little more. The British were inclined, therefore, to write off China in hopes that the Japanese threat could be staved off at least a year or so. Britain's policy was ascribable, of course, to her desperate situation in the summer of 1940. With France defeated and a German invasion threatening, it was feared that Japan could not resist the opportunity thus presented. In a less desperate time—as was to be seen in late 1941—Britain, when faced with a similar choice, decided to accept war with Japan rather than to see China go down. Later events made it apparent that Britain was not wedded to Munich diplomacy in the summer of 1940 but was balancing harsh alternatives in a time of extremity. It was also clear that the British would take a strong stand against Japan if the United States gave some evidence that military support would be forthcoming in the event of war. Such evidence Washington was unwilling to supply. The Australian Department for External Affairs advised the cabinet that if war came at this time American aid would not materialize,[19] and the British government was doubtless guided by the same assumption.

Several weeks lapsed before Britain fixed upon a policy. Within the Commonwealth there was much division of opinion. Sir Robert Craigie, the British Ambassador at Tokyo, urged London to offer Japan some alternative to aggression for which extremists and younger officers in Japan were pressing. He suggested British and United States cooperation to reach an understanding with Japan on a basis that included joint assistance to Japan in bringing about peace with China, peace founded on the restoration of China's independence and integrity. Australia agreed with Craigie's line of thought but believed that conditions including the independence and integrity of China would be quite impossible of acceptance by Japan. Menzies held that the immediate demands of Japan should be accepted.[20] The Chiefs of Staff at London recommended strongly that war not be risked on points not of vital importance to Britain. Rather, a general settlement should be sought with Japan.[21] Lord Halifax, the British Foreign Secretary, disagreed. He believed that resistance would not bring total war with Japan, and he favored resisting Japan's demands. He also pointed out the adverse effect the closing of the Burma Road would have upon American public opinion.[22] New Zealand likewise urged a firm stand against the Japanese.[23]

By the middle of July Britain had settled upon a policy midway between the divergent opinions. At the suggestion of Craigie, the War Cabinet decided to close the Burma Road for three months, a period when little traffic could be handled on the route due to the rainy season.[24] Shortly after the announcement of the British policy on July 14, Ambassador Lothian attempted to gain Hull's support, but the Secretary evidenced no sympathy for even this mild form of appeasement. On the contrary, he issued a public statement criticizing the "unwarranted interposition of obstacles to world trade."[25]

While Britain and Australia attempted to conciliate Japan, the United States, moving in the opposite direction, took a major step along the road of economic sanctions. In July, 1939, the United States had abrogated the United States-Japanese treaty of commerce, and now legislation was passed allowing the administration to apply progressive economic sanctions against Japan. On July 2 Congress adopted an act authorizing the President to prohibit or curtail the export of military goods and materials used in making such products. Roosevelt lost no time in using the legislation. On the day the bill was signed he issued a proclamation making the export of a long list of raw materials and machine tools subject to export licenses to be issued by the Secretary of State. Then on July 26 an embargo was placed on aviation gasoline and on high-grade iron and steel.[26]

The British, Australians, and Dutch evidenced concern that the embargo might force Japan to turn on the Indies, but these fears were premature. The restrictions were more significant as an indication of things to come rather than as an immediately effective blow at Japan's war economy. Initially the embargo applied only to aviation gasoline and the Japanese could produce this by using tetraethyl from Germany, Italy, Russia, or Mexico. In other grades of petroleum the Japanese were increasing their storage supplies. In the month of August, licenses were issued for the export to Japan of $21,000,000 worth of American petroleum products, more than the total for the entire first six months of the year. Regarding iron and steel, only the highest grade was embargoed, and Japan was importing most of the remaining seventy-five grades as rapidly as possible.[27]

The long-term significance of Washington's move was nevertheless profound. The embargo on aviation gasoline and high-grade iron and steel was the first step in a program of progressive economic sanctions. These sanctions, unlike their predecessors, the ineffective "moral embargoes," were backed by the full power of legality. In succeeding months the list of embargoed goods steadily lengthened until the policy reached its full implementation with oil sanctions in July, 1941. Within the Roosevelt administration counsels were divided as to the wisdom of sanctions and the degree to which they should be implemented. Ambassador Grew at Tokyo consistently opposed the policy of sanctions until he sent his so-called "green light" telegram to Washington in September, 1940; and even after that date he sometimes reverted to his previous position of opposing sanctions.[28] Within Roosevelt's cabinet Secretary of the Treasury Henry Morgenthau, Jr., and Secretary of the Interior Harold L. Ickes had long urged economic sanctions and sought to make them as strong as possible.[29] In July, 1940, the very month in which sanctions were implemented, Henry L. Stimson joined the cabinet as Secretary of War. Stimson, as Republican Secretary of State under Hoover, had at times recommended sanctions during the Manchurian crisis of 1931-1933; and after the eruption of the Sino-Japanese War in 1937 he had become an outspoken advocate of such a policy. He now joined Morgenthau and Ickes in urging a tough policy toward Japan.[30] Hull, though as bitter against Japan as any member of the cabinet, took a position midway between Grew and the advocates of drastic action. He did not share the belief of Morgenthau, Ickes, and Stimson that the Japanese would back down in the face of full economic sanctions. When the first sanctions were announced in July, 1940, their mild character was due to the influence of the Department of State which, at least initially, outmaneuvered the proponents of drastic action.[31] Hull was willing, however, that progressive sanctions be applied so that each Japanese move would be met by another turn of the economic screw.

Throughout August and into September of 1940 the Roosevelt administration debated the advisability of more effective sanctions. Canberra, meanwhile, asked London not to pursue a policy of conciliation to a point that would sacrifice American diplomatic cooperation. The Australian government emphasized that it was hostile to a policy of mere appeasement to Japan and that Australia accepted as axiomatic the advantage of a common policy in the Far East with the United States. Indeed, Australia informed the British government that a considerable modification of Empire policy would be justified in order to get American support in carrying through a joint or parallel policy.[32] In tendering these recommendations to London, the Australian government played an unusual role, for during 1940-1941 it was more often London that submitted such views to Canberra.

While Australia was counseling the home country not to follow a program of "mere appeasement," the British government was considering the adoption of a stiffer policy than either Washington or Canberra favored. This was evident during the Indochina crisis in August and September. Beginning in early August, Japan forced further demands upon the French, including the right to station six thousand troops in Tonkin and the right of passage through Tonkin to Yunnan, China, of additional troops (not to exceed twenty-five thousand). Airfields were to be constructed for the use of Japanese planes, and Indochina was to enter the Japanese Co-Prosperity Sphere.[33] On September 16, when the Franco-Japanese negotiations had reached a critical juncture, Lothian and Casey discussed the problem at length with Hull, and Lothian indicated that Britain was considering tendering substantial military aid to French Indochina. Hull was quite concerned at this new direction of British policy and attempted to dissuade the British from such a move. He stated that it was difficult to aid provinces to resist Japan when the mother countries could not do so. He also reminded Lothian that it would not be wise even from the British standpoint for two wars to rage simultaneously. Hull told Lothian and Casey at this time, however, that the United States intended to impose more and more economic retaliations on Japan.[34]

The Australian government did not indicate what stand it would take on military aid to Indochina until late September when Casey revealed that a decision had been made not to send even arms.[35] That decision had been foreshadowed early in August when the War Cabinet in Australia had discussed the question of aiding the Netherlands East Indies. At that time the Cabinet had ruled against entering a binding obligation to assist the Dutch, though it was realized that a Japanese attack would almost inevitably bring war between Australia and Japan.[36] In view of the refusal of the United States to pledge aid, Australia was reluctant to take as strong a stand against Japan as aid to Indochina implied. The United States gained a hint of Australia's position during the Indochina crisis when Casey told Assistant Secretary Berle on September 3 that he saw no particular purpose in sticking to the October 15 date for reopening the Burma Road.[37] Thus, by early September, in the vacillation of British policy, Australian influence was being exerted on the side of conciliation.

The British military aid to Indochina did not materialize, but just three days after the French capitulated to Japanese demands on September 22, the United States took the most drastic action yet undertaken against Japan. A complete embargo on all types of iron and steel scrap was announced, thus cutting off the main source of supply for one of Japan's key war materials.[38] "This is a direct hit at Japan," noted Secretary of War Stimson, "a point which I have hoped we would hit for a long time."[39]

If London or Canberra entertained any qualms about the drastic American action, they were immediately cancelled out by the signature on September 27, 1940, of the Tripartite Pact, which lodged Japan firmly in the Axis camp. Negotiations for the agreement had been transpiring intermittently since 1938, and now with the victories of Germany in Europe, Japan was encouraged to tie her destiny to the Nazi star. The pact was directed specifically at the United States, for the signatories undertook to assist one another with all political, economic, and military means if one were attacked by a power not then involved in the European war or in the Chinese-Japanese conflict. Russia, which might have been affected by this provision, was excluded from its application by another article of the treaty. Thus the United States was the obvious target of the treaty. Other provisions recognized the leadership of Germany and Italy in Europe and Japan in East Asia.[40]

Washington's response to the Tripartite Pact was typified by Secretary Hull. Publicly he announced that the agreement did not "substantially alter a situation which has existed for several years," but privately he betrayed an inclination to stiffen policy toward Japan. When he met with Lothian on September 30, he conversed in a more belligerent tone than usual. He said that Japan would find it necessary to assume that whether or not the United States and Britain had definite agreements with regard to naval and air bases across the Pacific to and including Singapore, the special relations between these two countries were such that they could overnight easily establish cooperative relations for the mutual use of these bases. He then inquired whether the British, Dutch, Australians, and New Zealanders had conferred on pooling their defense forces in case of danger.[41] Lothian's impression of America's stronger policy is contained in his own correspondence: "United States has become very near to war since the pact between the Axis and Japan. It's a challenge to U.S.A. and they know it. It wouldn't take much—a real insult or an attack on some vital interest to swing the United States over."[42]

The British and Australian reaction to the pact was evidenced in the decision to reopen the Burma Road when the three-month period ended in mid-October. Washington received the first inkling of this when Australian Minister Casey called on Assistant Secretary Berle on September 27, the day the pact was announced. Casey said that Lothian was in favor of opening the Burma Road and adopting a strong line. Casey took the opportunity, however, to question Berle regarding American support if war came. Though he did not press the Assistant Secretary for an answer, he posed the question of whether it might not be assumed that in the event that war resulted, the United States would "immediately assist by going to war with Japan."[43] This was a question Casey was to repeat on many occasions during 1940 and 1941.

The British decision was made on October 4. The British cabinet decided to reopen the Burma Road on October 17, thus ending the experiment in appeasement.

CHAPTER EIGHT

Singapore:
Focus of Strategic Differences

O<small>N THE HEELS</small> of the Tripartite Pact came an Anglo-Australian attempt to persuade the United States to send warships to Singapore. As this project was pressed upon Washington during October and November of 1940, the fundamental considerations guiding American policy since the fall of France became more apparent. The basic tenet of official American thinking was that the Pacific area was of secondary importance compared with the struggle in Europe and that all decisions should be made on the basis of what would best serve the cause of victory in Europe. Administration leaders knew that any undertaking must be within the framework of nonbelligerency until the American public was ready to accept full-scale participation in the war, but Roosevelt and his associates were willing to go far with measures "short of war" to aid Britain in Europe. The willingness of the Roosevelt administration to follow an interventionist course in the Atlantic and in Europe did not mean, however, that it would pursue a similar policy in the Pacific. This became pristinely clear as the British and Australians pleaded for an American demonstration at Singapore.

The British were apparently pondering a Singapore naval demonstration by the United States within a few days of the conclusion of the Tripartite Pact. While lunching on September 29 with Major James M. McHugh (U.S.M.C.), until recently assistant naval attaché at Chungking, Ambassador Lothian pointed out that even if Gibraltar, Suez, and Hong Kong fell, an American fleet could control the East-West trade routes from Singapore.[1] Then on October 4, when Churchill informed Roosevelt that the Burma Road would be reopened, he suggested an American naval visit to Singapore. "Anything in this direction," said the Prime Minister, "would have a marked deterrent effect upon a Japanese declaration of war upon us over the Burma Road opening." Regarding the size of the visiting squadron, he said "the bigger the better."[2]

The day after Churchill's proposal arrived in Washington, it was considered by a committee made up of Under Secretary Welles, Army Chief of Staff George C. Marshall, and Chief of Naval Operations Harold R. Stark. Their recommendation was that the visit not be undertaken. Such a move, they believed, might precipitate hostilities; in any case the Western Pacific was a theater of war second in importance to the Atlantic.[3] Several days later Roosevelt received directly opposite advice from Stimson. The Secretary of War recommended that the American fleet "establish itself at Singapore."[4]

Roosevelt was at this time pondering some alternative demonstration in the Pacific. On October 8 he asked Admiral William D. Leahy, former Chief of Naval Operations, whether he thought the reinforcement of the Asiatic Fleet at Manila would serve to deter the Japanese. Leahy conceded that such a gesture would have a temporary deterrent effect, but he warned that when war came in the Pacific the Asiatic Fleet might be lost and therefore only a few of the least valuable ships should be sent. However, Admiral James O. Richardson, the Commander in Chief of the Fleet, argued that not only should no demonstration be made in the Pacific, but the fleet should be withdrawn from Hawaii to the United States so that it could be properly prepared for war. A fleet that was unready for war, stated Richardson, could not be a serious deterrent to Japan.[5]

In late October the Roosevelt administration decided that no naval demonstration would be made in the Pacific but that the fleet would remain at Hawaii and limited measures would be taken to reinforce the Philippines. On October 23 the War Department announced that two squadrons of pursuit planes would be sent to the Philippines, and three weeks later the Navy ordered that ten additional submarines be based in the Islands.[6]

Both Australia and Britain continued to parley for a naval demonstration at Singapore. On November 12 Casey quizzed Hull on whether the United States contemplated a good-will naval mission to Australia and to "other countries in the southern areas," but Hull replied merely that his government had other plans in mind than a good-will mission.[7] Several days later Casey told Berle that his government hoped that the United States might send a naval force to visit Singapore but if this could not be done a "visit of courtesy" to Australia might be considered.[8] Then on November 25 Lothian, just returned from a visit to London, informed Hull that naval experts believed that if the American navy were headquartered largely at Singapore, it would safeguard the entire situation in the Orient.[9]

While the Australians and the British were pushing the Singapore project, they were also making parallel efforts to persuade the United States to participate in staff conferences at Singapore. The matter had been first broached on September 16 when Lothian suggested conferences in regard to bases and a unified defense effort from Singapore through the Australian area in the direction of the United States. Hull evidenced no enthusiasm for the project at that time,[10] but a few days after the announcement of the Tripartite Pact, he asked Lothian whether the British, Dutch, and other South Pacific governments had conferred about pooling their defense efforts. At that time Lothian had disclaimed any knowledge of these "technical matters,"[11] but in the subsequent weeks Lothian and Casey proceeded to press the United States to enter staff conferences at Singapore. Churchill, in his message to the President on October 4 urging the Singapore visit, also proposed staff conferences between British, Australian, Dutch, and American naval authorities at Singapore,[12] and on the following day Casey and Lothian stressed the project to Hull. The Secretary made it clear, however, that he was thinking in terms of Anglo-Australian-Dutch talks, and he suggested that Britain contact the experts of those countries.[13] Hull soon indicated, however, that though the Roosevelt administration was unwilling to discuss specifically the defense of Singapore, it was willing to undertake talks directly with the British government on world-wide strategy. On October 7 Hull told Lothian that British-American staff conferences should be conducted in Washington or London at as early a date as possible.[14]

British-Australian-New Zealand staff consultations were held at Singapore late in October, and these were followed by Anglo-Dutch conferences in December. As the sessions were getting underway at Singapore, the United States was asked to have the American consul general on hand as an observer, but the invitation was not accepted. The navy did, however, send the naval attaché from Thailand to keep in touch with the proceedings.[15] As the meetings progressed, it became grimly apparent to the participants how desperately defense measures were needed in the Far East. It was agreed that Singapore was the key to the Commonwealth defensive position and that Australia and New Zealand would be best defended by a concentration of forces in Malaya. It was also acknowledged that defense forces there were woefully inadequate. The conferees recommended that an R.A.F. strength of 582 aircraft be maintained in the area, but there were at that time only 88 first-line aircraft in Malaya. Participants also suggested that a defense force of twenty-six infantry battalions, five field regiments, and three light tank companies was required for the land defenses of Malaya—modest recommendations in the light of later events—but there were in Malaya only seventeen infantry battalions and one mountain regiment of mobile artillery.[16]

In the weeks following the Singapore conferences, little was done to remedy the deficiencies. The forces and equipment were simply not available. Australia and New Zealand were exerting their major military efforts in the Middle East, and Britain was fighting gallantly to turn back the *Luftwaffe* and counter the threat of invasion. The weakness at Singapore made it even more obvious that Britain and Australia must seek closer collaboration with the United States. At Washington, Casey had come forward with a plan for United States-Australian staff conferences, but his proposal was rejected, even though he took it personally to Roosevelt.[17] In the subsequent weeks Casey and Lothian contined to prod the United States to take up defense discussions with the South Sea countries.

The reluctance of the United States to become entangled in the defense of Singapore caused considerable anxiety among Australian leaders. After the announcement of America's scrap iron embargo in September, Australia had applied a similar embargo, and now Australians questioned the wisdom of that action. In December, Casey told Welles that Australia was not able to pursue a policy of economic sanctions against Japan with the same impunity as the United States. Casey said he regarded it as unwise for Australia to continue a policy of this character which brought the wrath of Japan down upon Australia without any resultant benefits to Australia therefrom.[18] Casey was reflecting an uneasiness that pervaded Australian government circles. If American policies placed Japan in a position where she either had to retreat or to plunge forward, Australians feared that she would strike to the south. In such a case the Japanese blow would surely fall upon the British Commonwealth; yet there was no assurance of American support in such a contingency. This consideration influenced Australian policy in varying degrees right up to December of 1941.

Throughout 1940 the British and Australian efforts to draw the United States into closer collaboration in the Far East were unsuccessful. The reasons for this were found in basic policies regarding the winning of the war, but there was a further factor in October, 1940, when Lothian and Casey were making their most vigorous efforts. The year 1940 was a presidential election year, and the electorate would go to the polls in November. The Roosevelt administration was keenly sensitive to the power of the isolationists, and this was particularly true so far as the Far East was concerned. The American public was indifferent to the importance of Far Eastern issues, and Roosevelt seemed exceedingly reluctant to pursue an interventionist policy, in that area. Any involvement in the defense of Singapore would likely bring the charge that American lives were being risked to uphold British imperialism in Asia. With Europe it was quite another matter. The American public seemed to realize that American security, as well as Britain's survival, was at stake in the struggle being waged on and across the Atlantic. Thus while the Roosevelt administration in September, 1940, was sending to Britain fifty destroyers in return for leases on bases in the Atlantic and the Caribbean—a flagrant violation of neutrality according to traditional concepts of international law—it was carefully refraining from staging a naval demonstration in the Far East. While Washington agreed to staff conferences with the British at Washington, it declined to participate in Anglo-Australian-New Zealand talks at Singapore.

Political considerations were not the only factor, nor indeed the major factor, in creating the seemingly paradoxical policy of intervention in Europe and isolation regarding the Far East. More important were basic views on strategy for winning the struggle against totalitarianism, and these considerations continued to dictate such a policy after Roosevelt won an unprecedented third term.

The strategic bases of American policy became quite apparent at the British-American staff conferences launched in Washington in January, 1941.

As early as October 7 Hull had informed the British that the United States would participate in British-American staff conferences in Washington or London. No efforts were made during October and November to effect the meeting, possibly because of the election, but at the end of November Roosevelt agreed to arrangements to conduct the talks in Washington. The death of Ambassador Lothian in December caused further delay, and the representatives of the British Chief of Staff did not arrive until late in January, 1941. The delegation, disguised as military advisers to the British Purchasing Commission, crossed the Atlantic on the battleship *George V*, the same ship that brought the new British ambassador, Lord Halifax. Hull had made it plain to the British before the conference began that the United States would not make any commitments on participation in the war, but the conference, which assembled on January 29, nevertheless represented an important progression toward intervention in the European war. However cautious the American stipulations, however scrupulously political officials abstained from attendance, the very subjects discussed possessed a deep significance. The staff conferences were meaningful only if it were assumed that the United States would eventually enter the war.

During the early sessions at Washington, the American delegates delineated the strategic considerations the United States believed should be followed in the eventuality that it became a belligerent. The principal effort, they stated, should be exerted in the Atlantic and navalwise in the Mediterranean. Every effort should be made to stave off Japan's entrance into the war, but if this proved impossible, American operations should not initially be on such a scale as to jeopardize the principal effort in the Atlantic. The British accepted the thesis that Europe was the most vital theater, but they insisted upon the importance of their Far Eastern position, including the security of Australia and New Zealand. Australia, whose representatives were present as members of the British delegation but not as official participants in the conference, strongly concurred.[19] Here the most serious difference of the entire conference emerged, for the British averred that Singapore was the key to their position in the East and asked that the United States assume some responsibility for its defense. The Americans were unable to accept the British position, and in the subsequent sessions the disagreement over Singapore emerged as clearly illustrative of a fundamental difference between the strategic conceptions of Britain and the United States.

British strategy, as outlined at the Washington meetings, was of a delaying and defensive type. No grand assault on Europe was contemplated until blockade and air bombardment had so reduced Germany's power that the invasion could be undertaken without staggering losses. This, admittedly, might require many months or years. Meanwhile Britain would maintain its other positions throughout the world in Malaya, North Africa, and the Middle East. American planners, on the other hand, conceived of an invasion of the continent as soon as the vast striking force could be assembled. Though American military leaders were painfully aware of present weaknesses, they were optimistic about the country's potential military strength. With America's immense power, an invasion could be planned in the foreseeable future, and thus all energies should be directed toward this blow. Singapore and other British outposts were considered expendable, for the decisive action against totalitarianism could be achieved only in the heart of Europe.[20]

The result was that no meeting of minds took place on Pacific strategy. The minutes recorded the deadlock succinctly: "It was agreed that for Great Britain it was fundamental that Singapore be held; for the United States it was fundamental that the Pacific Fleet be held intact."[21] Something of a compromise was nevertheless incorporated in the ABC-1 plan that emerged from the conference. The United States would strengthen its forces in the Atlantic and Mediterranean areas so that the British Commonwealth would be free to release the ships necessary to defend British territories in the Far East. The American Pacific Fleet's task was to be mainly defensive—the protection of American possessions in the Pacific—but it was also to undertake a diversion toward the Marshall and Caroline Islands to relieve pressure on the Malay Barrier.[22]

The basic Anglo-American difference over Singapore persisted throughout the conference and after the adjournment on March 27. American strategic thinking meanwhile was reflected in naval dispositions. Secretary of the Navy Frank Knox announced in January, 1941, that the United States Fleet would be divided into three forces: the Pacific Fleet, the Atlantic Fleet, and the Asiatic Fleet. In making the announcement Knox implied that if there were any withdrawal of strength from the Pacific Fleet, it would be added to the Atlantic Fleet. The Asiatic Fleet, stationed at Manila, would not be reinforced.[23]

Despite all the indications that the United States would not become involved in the defense of Singapore, Australia and the United Kingdom continued to advocate the ships-to-Singapore project. In February, 1941, Casey sent Hull a long list of statistics compiled by the Office of Public Opinion Research at Princeton University showing that over fifty per cent of the Americans polled thought the United States should risk war with Japan in order to prevent her from taking Singapore.[24] In the succeeding weeks Halifax continued to deliver telegrams from London bombarding Hull with requests to send ships to Singapore. To all the British and Australian pleas, the United States turned a deaf ear.

CHAPTER NINE

Courtship But No Concessions

W HILE basic strategic considerations were being thrashed out in the staff conversations in Washington, closer United States-Australian cooperation was being facilitated in Australia where the first United States minister, Clarence E. Gauss, had arrived in July, 1940. In this time of adversity the Australian government, so reluctant to open formal diplomatic relations, now seemed exceedingly glad to have this further channel for winning American friendship. John R. Minter, who accompanied Gauss to Canberra as First Secretary, said that the reception "has made quite an impression on us." "We knew the Australians were hospitable," he noted to friends at the Department of State, "but we did not expect so much."[1]

The first weeks of Gauss's stay in Australia were given over to the details of setting up the legation in Canberra, a task made difficult by the wartime housing shortage. The legation offices were finally established in a leased residence, Brigden house, and the legation personnel were obliged to lease separate residences.[2] The housing shortage, which continued to be a nuisance until the construction of a legation was undertaken in 1942, was not, however, the only difficulty encountered by Minister Gauss. More serious was the sheer physical hurdle of dealing with a government scattered in three different cities. When Parliament was not in session, the cabinet members resided principally in Melbourne and Sydney, and cabinet meetings were often held in Melbourne, at times in Sydney, and sometimes in other state capitals. The defense ministries were also located in Melbourne.[3]

The difficulties of operating a legation in Australia were offset by the good relationship between Gauss and Prime Minister Menzies.

Gauss was favorably impressed by Menzies. "He appears to me to be the ablest man that Australia can produce at this time," he wrote in a private letter to Moffat.[4] Gauss soon won the respect of Australian leaders, who took him into their confidence on matters affecting Australian foreign relations. The most significant development during his first months in Canberra was the appointment of an Australian minister to Japan. The announcement came in August, and was followed by much speculation as to how the appointment would affect Australia's policy toward Japan, for Sir John Latham, who had been delegated to open the new legation at Tokyo, was believed by some to be pro-Japanese. Before Latham left for Tokyo, however, he conferred at length with Gauss, and his remarks, Gauss reported, "failed to confirm the reports that he is pro-Japanese."[5] Among other things, Latham told Gauss that "we must all do what we can to keep China on Japan's back."[6]

During his relatively short tenure in Australia, Gauss strove to direct the developing United States-Australian rapprochement along what he considered realistic lines. That a rapprochement was underway was very apparent from the Australian vantage point. "Admiration for the United States grows daily," Gauss reported in September, 1940. "Every activity in the United States," he noted, "is followed with the keenest interest and there is evidence that political developments in the United States during the next few months are viewed as having almost as great significance for Australia as do Australian political developments themselves."[7] Two months later his report was even more emphatic: "There can be no doubt that the feeling generally throughout Australia is more friendly to the United States, at the moment, than it has been at any time since the two countries were associated in the World War."[8]

In 1940 Gauss and other observers could see that Australians were taking a greater and more sympathetic interest in American affairs. It would be easy, however, to overestimate the depth of the rapprochement and the extent to which the old attitudes and misunderstandings had been superseded. When C. Hartley Grattan visited Australia in 1940, he found Australians still clinging to impressions of America as a materialistic, capitalistic society. Grattan judged that culturally there was still "a vast amount of hard work to be done before the average Australian has ordinary tolerance and understanding of American life and thought."[9] Fred Alexander, an Australian scholar who visited the United States in 1940, made similar observations regarding Australian views. He discovered that although Australians knew more of America than Americans knew of Australia, the Australian knowledge rarely extended beyond the superficial things in American life. Since most of their insights into American culture had been derived through motion pictures it was understandable, Alexander noted, that Australians tended to picture American cities as filled with gangsters and American universities revolving around burly football coaches and glamourous coeds.[10]

Australian perception regarding America's Pacific policy was perhaps as hazy as knowledge of American culture and society. Grattan found during his tour in 1940 that Australians had little appreciation of the subtleties of the ideological stalemate between the United States and Japan. Rather, their preoccupation was over "when, where and over what the United States will fight."[11] The Australian public and even Australian leaders exhibited unconcern over the crucial role that China played in American policy. "It must be confessed," noted the *Round Table* in 1941, "that Australians have shown little inclination to face this issue of principle, or even to recognize the vital strategical part played by China as the fly-paper on which the Japanese army has been firmly stuck and to which it is directly in Australia's interest to make it adhere more closely yet."[12] Australian officials sometimes commented on the importance of China, such as Latham's quip about keeping China on Japan's back, but they also reverted occasionally to the old policy of conciliation toward Japan. In several statements in 1939 Prime Minister Menzies struck a distinct note of friendship to Japan.[13] In late 1940 the Australian Minister for the Army, Sir Percy Spender, announced in a speech at Singapore that Australia had no quarrel with Japan. This avowal caused considerable confusion among Australians, and the perplexity was heightened further when shortly thereafter the Minister for External Affairs, Sir Frederick Stewart, described Australia's relations with Japan as cordial.[14]

Some Australians thought they discerned a deep rationale in the Australian policy and proclaimed that it was based on more than a desire not to provoke Japan, that it was groping for a comprehensive Pacific settlement which would provide a basis for permanent peace and prosperity in the Pacific.[15] It is, however, difficult to see how any settlement could have been effected in the Pacific as late as 1940 except at the expense of China—and to the eventual peril of British, Australian, and American territories and interests. But hope for an overall settlement in the Far East persisted among Australian leaders. As late as March, 1941, Menzies was still talking of reaching agreement and a friendly relationship with Japan.[16]

However much Australians perceived or misconceived of American affairs and America's Pacific policy, there is little doubt that Americans knew even less of Australia. When Fred Alexander surveyed American opinion regarding Australia in 1940, he discovered that Americans had a friendly feeling toward Australians but that American views were not founded on solid information. A lady on the Pacific Coast inquired what the train service was like between Sydney and Wellington! "Few Americans," he noted, "might seek to tunnel the Tasman, but . . ."[17] Alexander nevertheless considered that the friendly attitude toward Australians prevalent throughout the United States might be turned to advantage. He had encountered what he believed to be a widespread and deeply rooted suspicion of British imperialism in the Far East. "It follows from this," he wrote after his return to Australia, "that Australians have an excellent opportunity to serve as interpreters of British policy to the people of the United States."[18]

Australian and United Kingdom leaders had already concluded that Australia might play a vital role in influencing American public opinion. This had been one of the considerations in sending an Australian minister to Washington. British Ambassador Lothian had noted in a letter to an Australian friend in December, 1939, "There are many things that an Australian or Canadian Minister can say and do in Washington which a British Minister cannot."[19] The Australian minister, Casey, was uniquely suited to fill the key slot in such a program. The forty-nine-year-old minister was well educated (Trinity College, Cambridge), handsome, a World War I hero, and he possessed an unusual facility for winning friends. By late 1940 Australia and the United Kingdom were concocting elaborate schemes to influence American opinion.

Washington first learned of the propaganda plans through Gauss. In November, 1940, detailed information reached the American minister revealing that the British Ministry of Information wished to enlist the aid of the Dominions and particularly Australia in trying to mold American opinion toward cooperation with the British Empire. Australia, the draft plan stated, was in a position to contribute tremendously in this endeavor, for she was non-European and thus not so suspect regarding Old World entanglements. As the program developed, visits to Australia by American publicists, legislators, churchmen, and others were to be encouraged. Australia was to be combed for individuals to tour America, addressing Rotary Clubs, women's organizations, and similar groups. The services of an American public relations firm were also to be acquired at an estimated cost of three hundred thousand dollars.[20]

Both Gauss and the officials at the Department of State took a dim view of the blueprints for propaganda activities in the United States. When in late December the Australian legation called the Department to request permission to open a Bureau of Information, the Department seized the opportunity to caution the legation against propagandist activities. In several frank conversations with Alan S. Watt, the First Secretary of the Australian legation, Robert B. Stewart of the Division of European Affairs transmitted Hull's views to Casey. Watt was informed that the Department knew of the comprehensive Australian plans and did not approve of certain aspects. Stewart pointed out that whatever good might be accomplished in winning favorable American public opinion would be gambled away should details of the plans come to light. Though the Department had no objections to the establishment of a Bureau of Information, Stewart told Watt bluntly, it did not want any propaganda bureau set up.[21] As a result of these conversations the Australian government abandoned the more elaborate facets of its program, limiting its efforts to a moderate information bureau and speechmaking by Casey.

At Canberra Gauss reinforced the Department's efforts to tone down the publicity campaign of the Australian government. In numerous conversations with prominent Australians, he reiterated the thesis that Australia should seek to promote Australia to the American people through better treatment of American interests rather than via propaganda. He directed the attentions of Australian leaders to the disparity in the situation, that while Australians thought principally in terms of winning American support through publicity, American interests in Australia wished concrete, practical evidences of Australia's desire for America's friendship.[22] Gauss represented accurately the opinions of many American concerns in Australia. When Sir Keith Murdock questioned the agent of one prominent American firm in Australia, the agent responded in no uncertain terms that American interests had been criticized and resented in Australia for many years, and it was futile for Australians to think that a few honeyed remarks could remedy the situation overnight. Publicity activities, Murdock was told, would not close the gap; they would neither convince Americans of Australia's sincerity nor correct the ingrained attitudes of a large portion of the Australian public.[23]

Several issues then pending presented the Australian government with opportunities to court American good will through specific concessions. One was a longstanding desire on the part of American interests to open direct radio-telegraph service between Australia and the United States. In 1931 the Radio Corporation of America had reached agreement with Amalgamated Wireless of Australia for the opening of the circuit, but the Australian government's refusal to issue the necessary license had blocked the project. The fact that all telegraph messages between the United States and Australia were routed through Canada and that British interests would suffer if direct service were opened no doubt accounted for the reluctance of the government to issue the license. In 1938 the United States government began to express interest in seeing direct service established, but the Australian government remained adamant.[24] In 1938 the Australian government consented to the opening of a direct radio-telephone circuit by American Telephone and Telegraph in cooperation with Amalgamated Wireless, but it refused to approve a direct radio-telegraph connection.[25] Gauss took up the matter with Menzies early in 1941, but was unable to convince the Prime Minister that Australia should seize the opportunity to win American good will by granting this specific concession.[26]

Gauss likewise made no headway on another pending issue. For several years Pan American Airways had sought landing privileges in Australia but had been denied them because the United States would not grant reciprocal landing rights at Honolulu for British aircraft. Gauss had no instructions to raise the matter officially with Canberra, but he did intimate to Menzies that a concession on this issue would boost Australian-American relations.[27] Menzies betrayed no inclination to make such a unilateral concession. Australia was apparently ready to do some horse trading, however, for Casey told a State Department official that Australia might rule favorably both on the radio-telegraph and on the Pan American issue, if landing permission in Hawaii and California could be granted to Britain.[28] The Department declined this bargain.

In early 1941, when Ambassador Nelson Johnson requested a transfer from China, the Department of State arranged for its two Far Eastern experts, he and Gauss, to exchange posts. Until Gauss left for Chungking in March, 1941, he continued to urge Australian leaders to build friendship, not through publicity but by "a fundamental examination of trade relations, communications, et cetera"; and he remained skeptical of Casey's publicity efforts in the United States. "I know that there is a substantial group in Australia," Gauss reported to Hull just prior to his departure, "that shares the view that the present propaganda program is shallow and deficient, and that Australia should look deeper and consider basic American-Australian problems."[29]

In the subsequent months Australia continued to rely upon Casey's speechmaking and upon the information bureau to forge bonds between the United States and the Commonwealth rather than upon affirmative action on various American requests. Minter, who served as chargé until the arrival of Nelson Johnson in August, chalked up no success in breaking the Pan American Airways or radio-telegraph deadlocks. A number of factors impeded agreement on the landing rights issue. Pan American had inaugurated service to Auckland, New Zealand, in 1940, and the New Zealand government feared that Auckland would be bypassed if landing privileges in Australia were granted to the airline. The Australian government, not wishing to damage New Zealand, numbered this consideration among its reasons for not allotting landing permission. Australia also continued to insist upon reciprocal rights for British planes at Hawaii, and chances were slight that the United States would accede to this demand. Pan American clippers used the naval base at Honolulu, no other landing base being available, and both the War and Navy departments were opposed to the British being allowed to land there. The Department of State was aware, too, that the right to land in Hawaii was a valuable concession, since it would be the last link in Britain's round-the-world air service. Therefore, it was adjudged a "very poor bargain" to exchange the concession at Hawaii in return for landing rights in Australia.[30] The entire matter was destined to drag on until after the outbreak of the Pacific War. Not until August, 1942, was Pan American finally allowed to open service to Sydney as a war measure and then under contract with the United States Navy.[31]

Various complications also prevented Minter from concluding a radio-telegraph agreement. One factor was the rivalry between the Australian Post Office Department and Amalgamated Wireless. Officials at the Post Office Department preferred to handle all overseas communications and thus opposed the issuing of a license to Amalgamated Wireless, despite the fact that the government owned fifty-one per cent of the stock in that company.[32] In addition, the Australian government had signed an agreement with the Imperial Cables and Wireless company guaranteeing to protect that system from outside competition. In 1941 that contract had two years to run.[33] The United States made several representations to London and to Ottawa on one occasion hoping to overcome the resistance of the British company,[34] but by late 1941 the situation was still unresolved. Political authorities in both Britain and Canada were amenable to the opening of the circuit, but the Australian government was reluctant to issue the license to Amalgamated Wireless without the consent of Imperial Cables and Wireless.[35] The deadlock was not broken until after the attack on Pearl Harbor. On December 13 Hull cabled Canberra that the telegraphic circuit was "absolutely imperative."[36] Three days later the Australian government consented to the project, and on December 25 the circuit was opened.[37]

While Gauss and Minter were struggling unsuccessfully for concessions at Canberra, Casey was achieving a large measure of success in the United States in his efforts to win friendship and aid for the British Commonwealth. During 1940 and 1941 he made major addresses almost every month which were widely publicized. In March, 1940, he spoke to the National Press Club in Washington, D.C. In April he addressed the Economic Club of New York at a meeting presided over by Wendell L. Willkie. In late June he was the featured speaker at "Australia Day" at the New York World's Fair. Later in the year he spoke to the New York *Herald Tribune* Forum. In January, 1941, he addressed the Boston Chamber of Commerce. The following month he expressed his views in a feature article in the New York *Times* Sunday edition. In June he journeyed to California to speak at the commencement exercises of the California Institute of Technology. The next month he was one of the featured speakers at the University of Virginia's Institute of Public Affairs.[38]

Casey's first speeches were carefully worded addresses which stressed the efforts and sacrifices being made by Australia and Britain in the war against Nazi tyranny. During 1941, however, he began to bear down hard on America's stake in the war, pointing out how the survival of free institutions in the British Commonwealth and the preservation of British sea-power were vital to the United States. When he gave a radio address from Washington in July, 1941, he frankly told Americans that his country had not gone into the war because of some European dispute. Australia had gone in because it realized that if it did not stand by Britain and throw itself across the track of the Nazi juggernaut, the democratic way of life would be lost. It was no more "Britain's war," he told his American listeners, than it was "your war." Two months later when he addressed the American Legion convention in Oklahoma, he all but told his audience that if the preservation of democracy was of vital significance to the United States, it should enter the war.[39]

Gauss's predictions that Australia's publicity activities would be no adequate substitute for concessions in the diplomatic arena proved to be wrong. Even American diplomats had to eventually concede—albeit grudgingly—that Casey's work was successful. Moffat, now serving as minister at Ottawa, wrote to Minter in August, 1941: "Australia has a remarkable press in the United States and Casey has done a unique job in the United States. At times I think he has tended to over-play his cards, but by and large he has put Australia on the map."[40]

CHAPTER TEN

American Cruisers Visit Australia

THE FIRST WEEKS of 1941 saw the beginning of a serious war scare. Reports of Japanese preparations for an immediate attack southward flooded Canberra, London, and Washington during January and early February. Ambassador Grew cabled from Tokyo on January 9 that one of his colleagues who possessed Axis contacts had informed him that Japan planned a general invasion of Indochina in late February.[1] Shortly after Grew's report, the British ambassador at Tokyo cabled rumors of Japanese plans to attack British possessions in late February in conjunction with a German invasion of England.[2] At the end of January the Australian minister at Tokyo reported that units of the Japanese fleet were in the Gulf of Siam and were expected to enter the harbor of Saigon.[3] In early February the Admiralty informed the American naval attaché at London that the Japanese apparently were organizing a largescale offensive, to be mounted presumably against Indochina, the Malay Peninsula, or the Dutch East Indies in conjunction with a German attack on Great Britain about February 10.[4] On February 7 more ominous intelligence lent credence to the rumor. The British government informed the United States that the Japanese embassy in London had received instructions to prepare to leave on short notice.[5] In Australia, cable messages to Japanese firms abroad from Japan were intercepted. These ordered the firms to reduce staffs and send home all who were not required, particularly women.[6]

As anxieties over the outbreak of a Pacific war intensified, the British government undertook a concerted effort to obtain some demonstration of American support. "The only thing likely to

98

avert war," the Foreign Office cabled Halifax, "is to make it clear to Japan that further aggression will meet with the opposition both of the United States and of ourselves." Foreign Secretary Anthony Eden knew there was little chance of securing a joint declaration to that effect, so in addition to proposing such a joint statement he suggested several alternatives. One course of action might be a strong warning by Roosevelt when he received the new Japanese ambassador, Admiral Kichisaburo Nomura. Eden thought, however, that the most effective check upon the Japanese would be "some definite move on the part of the American Fleet."[7] In a personal message to Roosevelt on February 16, Churchill pointed out that any threat of a major invasion of Australia and New Zealand would force Britain to withdraw her fleet from the Eastern Mediterranean, opening possibilities for disastrous military reverses there. "Everything that you can do to inspire the Japanese with fear of a double war," Churchill urged, "may avert the danger."[8]

The British received substantial support from the United States. Eden had already on February 7 informed the Japanese that Britain would defend her possessions in the Far East with vigor,[9] and Roosevelt proceeded in turn to press caution upon the Japanese. Meeting with Ambassador Nomura on February 14, he told him Americans were so indignant over Japanese aggression that an incident like the sinking of the *Maine* in 1898 might precipitate war.[10] Tokyo received an even stronger warning from the Counselor of the American embassy at Tokyo, Eugene Dooman. Dooman told the Japanese Vice Minister for Foreign Affairs, Chuichi Ohashi, that if Japan were to prejudice the safety of British communications between Britain and the British dominions and colonies overseas, either by direct action or by placing herself in a position to menace those communications, conflict with the United States could be expected. Ohashi, somewhat stunned by this, queried, "Do you mean to say that if Japan were to attack Singapore there would be war with the United States?" Dooman replied, "The logic of the situation would inevitably raise that question."[11]

Dooman's stern admonition was delivered without instructions from Washington and asserted more than Washington wished to say at this time, but his action was not disavowed and it made a profound impression at Tokyo. Ambassador Grew himself reinforced Dooman's words by handing to Foreign Minister Yosuke Matsuoka a copy of the memorandum of the Dooman-Ohashi conversation.[12] While these warnings bombarded Tokyo, officials at Washington undertook discussions concerning a possible naval demonstration in the Pacific.

In Australia the rumors of war engendered great anxiety. The public, though not aware of the disturbing diplomatic reports, observed many danger signs. Japan was known at this time to be using a Thailand-French Indochina border dispute to extend her influence over Thailand. On February 10 Royal Air Force bombers departed Singapore to reinforce advance bases in northern Malaya along the border with Thailand. Then came hurried meetings of the Advisory War Council. Menzies was enroute to London for consultation when the war scare flared up, and the Council, meeting in his absence, issued alarming statements. Arthur Fadden, the Acting Prime Minister, and John Curtin, the leader of the Labour opposition, released a joint statement on February 13 stating that the war had "moved on to a new stage involving the utmost gravity."[13] Two days later Casey told Hull that the danger to his country was steadily increasing.[14]

Within a few days of Casey's expression of concern to Hull, the anxieties over war started to subside. British and Australian leaders perceived, and correctly so, that Japan did not plan an advance at this time. Churchill cabled Roosevelt on February 20, "I have better news about Japan."[15] Reports from the Australian minister at Tokyo also indicated that no attack by Japan was imminent.[16] The relaxation in tension which soon settled over London and Canberra was not entirely shared by Washington. Initially, United States officials had been less quick than Commonwealth leaders to believe the rumors of war, but their anxiety persisted longer. When in early March the British brought news of reassuring statements by Matsuoka, the State Department's political adviser, Stanley K. Hornbeck, noted: "We are somewhat surprised at Sir Robert Craigie's acceptance, apparently without question or challenge, of Matsuoka's repeated affirmation to the effect that Japan has not been sending (large) reenforcements southward." "Is there not ample evidence," Hornbeck asked rhetorically, "that Japan has within recent weeks sent a substantial number of transports southward and that a substantial number of Japanese cruisers are in waters along the south coast of China and the coast of Indochina?"[17]

The war scare of February, 1941, underscored once more the curious dichotomy in Australian thinking which had dogged Australian leaders and, to some extent, the Australian public throughout the 1930's. Many Australian leaders, including Prime Minister Menzies, prided themselves on taking a positive, constructive attitude toward the problem of Japan. This was a position that was difficult to reconcile with the harsh realities, particularly after the European war opened up such tempting opportunities to Japan. But hope died hard. In early March, while Hornbeck and others in Washington were pondering the continuing signs of danger, Prime Minister Menzies made a speech in London which seemed to cut across the rumors of war and point to friendship with Japan. At a luncheon of the Foreign Press Association Menzies voiced his belief that the Pacific could be made pacific if the peoples who lived on its borders were frank, sensible, and tolerant in understanding each other. No difficulty existed between nations, he said confidently, that could not be resolved by the cultivation of the utmost frankness. "Don't let us become victims of the very pernicious habit of believing that a possible conflict becomes inevitable," he concluded. "We aimed and are aiming at getting nearer to Japan."[18]

The timing of Menzies' remarks lifted eyebrows not only in London but in Canberra and Washington as well. He appeared to be rebuking the Australian leaders who had recently issued the ominous statements during his absence. The Sydney *Morning Herald* noted that Menzies apparently was attempting to pour oil over troubled waters but that his speech, which was not fortunately phrased, might be interpreted as implying that the waters were not troubled at all. "In his commendable anxiety to improve a delicate situation," said the *Herald*, "Mr. Menzies would seem to have fallen into the error of minimizing its seriousness, to the bewilderment of public opinion in Australia and in contradiction of his own assertion that there should be no pretense about international relations."[19] J. A. Beaseley, a Labour member of the Advisory War Council, charged Menzies with urging appeasement and observed caustically that there should not be two voices speaking at different ends of the earth on matters vital to Australia.[20] Curtin, the leader of the Labour party, publicly reminded Menzies of the unhappy realities:

> I say that nobody—not even the Prime Minister can escape the fact that an aggressor is on the move in regions affecting Pacific countries. Until the aggressor stops moving it would be a major blunder for any Australian to disregard the strategic potentialities of the position.[21]

While Menzies and Labour party leaders carried on their long-distance wrangle over policy toward Japan, the United States determined to proceed with a project that had been vigorously debated during the war scare, a naval demonstration in the South Pacific. Hull, who was usually cautious, had become convinced that such a step should be taken. Admiral Harold R. Stark, Chief of Naval Operations, opposed the project, fearing that commitments or dispositions in the Pacific would weaken the navy in the Atlantic,[22] but in March Roosevelt and Hull decided to send cruisers to Australia, New Zealand, Tahiti, and the Fiji Islands. On March 13 the United States asked the Australian government if two cruisers and five destroyers might call at Sydney on March 20-23 and Brisbane on March 25-28.[23] Canberra lost no time in welcoming the projected visit. Indeed, Australia would have been happy to extend hospitality to the entire United States Navy at this critical juncture.

While the Australian government launched secret preparations for the naval visit, another development occurred which greatly strengthened the developing Australian-American rapprochement. On March 11 the Congress passed the Lend-Lease Bill by which the United States committed its financial as well as its industrial resources to the Commonwealth's struggle. Acting Prime Minister Fadden told the House that the document would become "as vital for us and for our children as the Magna Charta and the Bill of Rights." He went on to tender Australia's profound thanks for the "great gesture of friendship" and for the "renewed strength" which the American people gave to Australia.[24] Later in the year Britain diverted some of the lend-lease aid to Australia, and in November, 1941, President Roosevelt declared Australia vital to the defense of the United States, thus enabling shipments to go directly from the United States to Australia. By March 31 1942, lend-lease aid to Australia totaled over thirty-seven million dollars.[25]

Arrangements for the naval visit were shrouded in secrecy until the day before the arrival of the ships at Sydney. News of the arrival thus broke with great suddenness. The official Parliamentary reception for the new Japanese Minister, Tatsuo Kawai, had been scheduled for 5 P.M., March 19, and just one hour before the reception took place the Parliament adjourned in order that ministers and members might proceed to Sydney to welcome the American ships. Thus the Japanese Minister had to content himself with some hasty handshaking as the members scurried to Sydney.[26]

From the moment the two cruisers (the *Chicago* and *Portland*) and five destroyers (the *Clark, Cassin, Conynham, Downes,* and *Reid*) steamed into the harbor of Sydney on March 20, the visit was a great success. At noon on the first day over half a million people elbowed and jostled each other to witness six hundred marines and sailors and six hundred men of the Australian armed forces march through the center of the city. Tons of torn paper, confetti, and streamers poured and looped from buildings as the troops paraded by. After the parade Acting Prime Minister Fadden set the keynote of the visit in his welcoming address:

> We welcome you as our cousins. We welcome you as people from the other side of the Pacific, who have extended to us not only the hand of friendship, but also the hand of practical support and cooperation. Nothing in the life of Australia has so stirred, inspired, and thrilled the nation as has this visit of part of the great United States Navy, synchronising with the wonderful action and works of President Roosevelt.[27]

For three days at Sydney and then three more days at Brisbane, enthusiastic Australians feted and honored Rear Admiral John Henry Newton and his officers and men.

The naval visit elicited a tremendous response in Australia. "The Navy," Minter reported to Hull, "was greeted [by the Australians] as if it were their own returning from a great victory." "To my mind," he said, "while I saw street demonstrations which I did not believe possible in Australia, the most striking event of the entire visit was the adjournment of Parliament and the trek of the entire government to Sydney."[28] Consul Doyle at Sydney re-

ported with equal enthusiasm. Coming only a few weeks after
Fadden's warnings to the nation of the imminent peril confronting
Australia, Doyle noted, "the visit struck Sydney with a powerful
perfectly-timed impact."[29] So warm and demonstrative was the
Australian reception that it amazed the Australians themselves.
Many Australians confided to Minter their surprise that their own
countrymen could wax so enthusiastic as to throw confetti or to
rush police cordons and wave flags.[30] Several days after the Sydney visit Minter reported that Fadden had not yet lost his enthusiasm. Minter attended the "Greek Day Appeal" on March 25 in
Canberra, and on that occasion the Acting Prime Minister dwelled
so long on the United States that someone remarked to Minter aft-
erward that "Artie apparently thought he was still welcoming the
fleet."[31]

CHAPTER ELEVEN

Australia Seeks Assurance
of American Aid

W HEN Harry Hopkins went to London early in 1941 as Roosevelt's personal representative, he found British leaders greatly concerned about whether the United States would come to Britain's aid if war came in the Pacific. "Eden asked me repeatedly what our country would do," Hopkins later recorded, "if Japan attacked Singapore or the Dutch East Indies, saying it was essential to their policy to know."[1] If this question preyed on the minds of British leaders, it troubled Australian leaders even more. The war scare of February, 1941, made Australians more fearful than ever of the outbreak of a Pacific war, and the visit of American cruisers, though reassuring, could not allay those fears.

Prime Minister Menzies was in London when Harry Hopkins was being quizzed by British leaders. Menzies' own anxieties were multiplied as a result of his talks with British leaders. In August, 1940, Churchill had assured Australia that if Japan set about invading Australia that Britain would cut her losses in the Mediterranean and send a fleet able to parry the invading force,[2] but Menzies now found British leaders raising practical obstacles to the carrying-out of this pledge. "It was stressed to me," Menzies cabled Australia in March, 1941, "that such a step would not be practicable until after the lapse of a considerable period, and might not be possible even then." The Chiefs of Staff in London considered that Britain's position in the Middle East remained essential to her strategy for the defeat of Germany, and even if the Mediterranean interests were abandoned, the fleet would have to remain during a long period of withdrawal. When Menzies returned to Australia three months later, he reported to the War Cabinet, "it is now evident that, for too long, we readily accepted the general assurances about the defence of this area."[3]

In April, 1941, Australian anxieties were heightened still further by news of the Russo-Japanese neutrality pact. Returning to Tokyo from talks with Axis leaders, Foreign Minister Matsuoka stopped by Moscow and negotiated the pact in conferences with Molotov. By its terms the signatories agreed that if either became an object of hostilities on the part of one or more third powers, the other would observe neutrality. It was apparent to Washington and Canberra that Japan was attempting to secure the Manchurian flank in preparation for the southward advance. If the full story had been known, the pact would have aroused even more uneasiness in those capitals. As early as February, 1941, Ambassador Hiroshi Oshima at Berlin had told German Foreign Minister Joachim von Ribbentrop that preparations for the assault on Singapore would be completed by the end of May. Moreover, in January, 1941, the commander of the combined fleets had approved a detailed plan for an attack on Pearl Harbor and actual training for the operation was to begin in May.[4]

The announcement of the Russo-Japanese pact stirred Australia to a concerted effort to secure at least a partial commitment from the United States for aid in the Pacific. Menzies persuaded British leaders at London to plunge wholeheartedly into an effort to obtain a declaration of support which might deter Japan.[5] On April 19, less than a week after the conclusion of the Russo-Japanese pact, Ambassador John G. Winant at London cabled an appeal from Eden. The Foreign Secretary urged the United States not to limit its consideration of Singapore to a purely tactical approach but to recognize its true political importance.[6] Three days later Halifax and Casey formally requested the issuance of a joint statement stipulating that, in the eventuality Japan moved further south, the interests of the United States, the British Empire, and the Netherlands would be jointly affected.[7] Hull evidenced no enthusiasm for the proposal. He reminded Halifax and Casey that he had already issued a pronouncement some months earlier when Japan was threatening the Dutch East Indies, and added that he did not concur in the idea of a joint statement. He did agree, nevertheless, to give further consideration to a possible parallel statement.[8] Later the same day Casey dispatched a separate appeal to Hull from the Australian government suggesting a joint declaration.[9]

In the succeeding days neither a joint nor a parallel statement materialized. On April 28 Hull discussed the subject with Casey and made it clear that the United States would not pursue the project. Hull said that he believed actions rather than words were decidedly more significant at the present stage. He noted that wide publicity was accorded the frequent conferences among himself, Casey, and Halifax and that these reports, together with the United States' own efforts to communicate its views to Japan, were ample so far as words were concerned. Public warnings to Japan, he said, might play into the hands of the extremists in Japan. Those leaders, said Hull, would be impressed only by definite actions, such as the recent visit of the American naval vessels to Australia.[10]

While Hull resisted involvement in the Far East, the United States was advancing toward intervention in the European war. On April 9 the United States assumed the protection of Greenland. Then on April 25 Roosevelt announced an even more significant step. The Navy would patrol the Atlantic as far as 26° west longitude (just west of Iceland) and would publish the position of possible aggressor ships or planes.[11] In other words, the United States Navy would hunt German submarines and upon finding them would call upon the British Navy to carry out their destruction. In Australia this further American commitment was applauded. Menzies, on his return to Australia, stated before the House that Roosevelt's Atlantic patrol was "one of the most remarkable happenings in this war." The eyes of a "great and friendly power," he said, had been added to Empire eyes in searching out U-boats.[12]

As the patrol measures in the Atlantic were put into motion, some administration leaders advocated shifting the Pacific Fleet to the Atlantic. Both Secretary of War Stimson and Secretary of the Navy Knox favored the transfer. Roosevelt and Hull, however, were reluctant to remove the deterrent in the Pacific. When Roosevelt consulted Churchill, the British Prime Minister thought at first that the shift should be made, but after reviewing the matter with Australia and New Zealand he asked that at least six capital ships be retained at Hawaii. When the issue was settled at the White House on May 6, it was decided that only three of the nine battleships at Pearl Harbor would be transferred to the Atlantic.[13]

While the United States was becoming more deeply embroiled in the Atlantic, conferences taking place at Singapore again revealed America's preoccupation with the Atlantic theater. The United States, it will be recalled, had refused to join in conferences at Singapore in October, 1940. When additional conferences were held in February, 1941, the United States had again refused to participate. Now, in April, 1941, Washington agreed to send representatives to conferences at Singapore, but exhibited the same reluctance to assume any commitments or approve any plans for Pacific defense that would detract from the struggle in the Atlantic. At the meetings conducted on April 21-27 the United States representatives, Capt. William R. Purnell and Col. Allan C. McBride, told the representatives of Australia, New Zealand, Britain, and the Netherlands that the United States could not commit itself in the Pacific. Specifically, the United States would not send ships to Singapore and would not further reinforce the Philippines. The ABD plan which emerged from the conference was rejected by the United States. The American army and navy chiefs considered that it spanned too wide an area (Africa to New Zealand) and that there was a danger that the Commander-in-Chief of the United States Asiatic Fleet, as the principal naval officer directly under the Commander-in-Chief of the British Eastern Fleet, might be ordered to operate in waters of no strategic significance to the United States and that too small a portion of the British naval forces in the Netherlands East Indies was allocated to support the United States Asiatic Fleet.[14]

During the first four months of 1941 there was, therefore, no basic change in American strategic conceptions regarding the Pacific. If war came in that area, no commitment bound the United States to participate, and, if American intervention did develop, first priority for troops and supplies was to be reserved for the European war.

The reluctance of the United States to become involved in a Pacific war was the major factor dictating the decision of the Washington government to undertake comprehensive diplomatic talks with Japan early in 1941. (These conversations began in January and continued, with one interruption, until the attack on Pearl Harbor.) The chances for a Japanese-American agreement were exceedingly small—Hull rated it one chance in a hundred—but the United States was eager to prevent or at least to postpone the outbreak of war in the Pacific if at all possible.

In the Japanese-American talks the governments of Australia and the other interested nations (New Zealand, Britain, and the Netherlands) played only a small part. Indeed, the American desire for secrecy was so strong that those governments received no clue as to the nature of the talks for many weeks, and not until November, 1941, were they made privy to the details of the exchange of communications. Casey and the other representatives thus were placed in an awkward position in their talks with the Department, for they could only speculate about what was happening in talks that were of vital concern to their countries. This state of affairs led to a misunderstanding in late May, 1941. The London government sent a note to the Department expressing concern over a possible American-sponsored Munich in the Far East, and Hull took great offense at the British implication.[15]

Actually there was little danger of a Far Eastern Munich, for in talks with Japan the United States was caught in a dilemma. In the near future Japan was clearly going to move southward unless an agreement could be concluded. But what kind of agreement would Japan accept? It was obvious throughout the discussions that Japan would accept only an agreement that would crown the China incident with success and leave Japan freer to undertake adventures elsewhere. The only serious impediment to the Japanese southward advance at this time was the commitment in China, and Chinese resistance by 1941 was in serious danger of collapsing. If the United States extended any substantial concession to Japan, such as a relaxation of economic sanctions, China likely would go down. In this event the United States would hold only Japan's paper promise not to march south, while Japan would have an enhanced position for aggression. The first Japanese draft indicated plainly that Japan was interested only in an agreement which would have this result. It was proposed that the United States force China to negotiate peace with Japan by threatening discontinuance of aid, that normal trade relations be restored between the United States and Japan, and that the United States help

Japan secure oil and other products from the Southwest Pacific area. In return Japan offered only a guarantee of the independence of a neutralized Philippines.[16]

While the Japanese-American talks were getting underway, Prime Minister Menzies visited Washington en route from London to Australia. He conferred with both Hull and Roosevelt concerning the Pacific question, but most of the discussion related to the progress of the British in Europe. Only one concrete proposal emerged from the conferences. Hull suggested that preliminary conversations for a trade agreement be reopened, and Menzies assented.[17] Some trade discussions were held at Washington later in the year, but as in the past no progress was made. The taking-up of the issue in 1941, however, provided an insight into the status of United States-Australian relations. In meetings conducted after Menzies returned to Canberra, it was apparent that despite the developing rapprochement trade matters were still an irritating factor. In a conversation with J. Frank Murphy, Secretary in the Department of Commerce, Chargé Minter expressed sentiments that still lingered in American official circles. Australia, he said, was "always looking for something from the United States without ever having given a thought to *quid pro quo*." Murphy admitted that it was probably one of the greatest anomalies of modern commercial relations that the United States at this time was the only country in the world suffering tariff discriminations by a country which it had declared itself willing to assist to the bitter end.[18]

Washington and Canberra soon were plagued by more critical matters than trade relations, for in July, 1941, Japan made the first major advance to the south. In late June Hitler had attacked Russia and had pushed Japan to invade Siberia. At an Imperial Conference on July 2, however, Japan decided to move south rather than against Russia. Ten days later Tokyo presented Vichy with an ultimatum demanding bases in southern Indochina. Then on July 24 Japanese troops occupied the bases.[19] Roosevelt immediately broke off the Washington conversations and issued a warning to Japan. He told Japanese Ambassador Kichisaburo Nomura that if Japan attempted to seize the oil supplies of the Netherlands East Indies, the Dutch would resist, the British Commonwealth would immediately assist the Dutch, "and, in view of our own policy of assisting Great Britain, an exceedingly serious situation would immediately result." The President then proposed the neutralization of Indochina.[20]

In the meantime the United States and the United Kingdom prepared to freeze Japanese assets and virtually end all trade with Japan. Australia concurred in the Anglo-American proposals but did so on the understanding that the United States would move first. There was concern in Canberra that the action might provoke war with Japan, and the government again proposed that an effort be made to secure a definite commitment from the United States. On July 25 Menzies cabled London the following message:

> It seems to us entirely feasible that in notifying the readiness of the British Commonwealth to concert with the United States in proposed economic action, the British Ambassador should intimate that we clearly realise the possible consequences of action, both for ourselves and the Netherlands, and that we assume that the United States Government also realises them. In a discussion which will arise on this basis, an indication of the United States' attitude will certainly appear. The nature of this in all probability will constitute the satisfactory understanding which we feel to be essential. We consider it vital, however, that the question should be raised in one form or another.[21]

On the day following Menzies' cable, Roosevelt froze Japanese assets in the United States, bringing all financial and trade transactions under government control. The United Kingdom did not think it advisable, nor was there time, to seek the guarantee of armed support which Australia desired, and the Commonwealth governments swiftly took action parallel to that of the United States.[22]

For several days the Roosevelt administration wavered in applying the freezing order. In Washington and throughout the Commonwealth there was a clear appreciation of the meaning of a combined embargo. Within a short time the production of Japanese industry would decline. Ton by ton Japan would have to draw on her limited reserve of oil. Roosevelt finally decided on a stiff policy, though not a complete embargo. Licenses might be issued, national defense needs permitting, for as much low-grade gasoline and crude oil as Japan bought in 1935-1936. Virtually no other trade, except in cotton and food, was to be allowed. As the weeks passed by, however, no licenses for oil were, in fact, issued.[23] Australia also decided to implement all-embracing sanctions which would be crippling in effect.[24] The Dutch, too, applied a complete oil embargo.[25] Within Japan the sense of crisis mounted. As Herbert Feis has observed, "From now on the oil gauge and the clock stood side by side. Each fall in the level brought the hour of decision closer."[26]

With the adoption of drastic economic sanctions the Australian government renewed its efforts to secure a commitment from Washington. On July 30 Menzies cabled London and the Dominion Prime Ministers:

> If the Americans feel in their hearts that in the event of warlike retaliation by Japan they could not remain aloof from the conflict, surely they can be made to see that a plain indication by them to Japan at this stage would probably avoid war. I recognize the traditional reluctance of the United States to enter into outside commitments in advance, but where the commitment seems inevitable, there is everything to be gained by promptly accepting it, and everything to be lost by delay. There is an apprehension in our minds and in the minds of leading members of the Opposition that the dangers in the Pacific are more dimly perceived elsewhere than by ourselves. We, vividly conscious of these dangers, are still convinced that the United States Administration is in the best position to dispel them.[27]

On August 2 Casey and Halifax urged Acting Secretary of State Welles to warn Japan against occupying Thailand, but Welles merely replied that the President had already extended his neutralization proposal to Thailand on July 31.[28] Two days later Halifax received a more encouraging statement from Welles. The Acting Secretary stated that though no definite commitment could be made, the United States would probably come to the aid of the Commonwealth in a Pacific war. If Japan attacked Singapore and the East Indies, he asserted, a situation would be created which could not be tolerated by the United States. "By this I said," Welles recorded in his memorandum of the conversation, "I meant that such a situation as that in my judgment would sooner or later inevitably result in war with Japan. I said that Lord Halifax was fully familiar with our constitutional system and that consequently no definite commitments or threats to this effect could officially be made."[29]

Welles's statement and his own interpretation of it summed up precisely the position of the Roosevelt administration in August,

1941. But despite the presence of obvious "constitutional difficulties," Australia continued to seek a commitment. When Hull returned from a rest cure at White Sulphur Springs, West Virginia, in early August, Casey came to the Department to question him on the probable reaction of the United States if Japan started a Pacific war. Hull could only reply that what the United States might do depended on the situation of the British in their struggle against Hitler and the particular circumstances and conditions both in the Pacific and the Atlantic presenting themselves at the time.[30] Shortly thereafter he repeated the same thing to Halifax and added that in the event of further Japanese advances, the British and Americans should confer at once and determine what further measures to employ.[31]

With the United States' refusal to be pinned to a commitment, Australian leaders considered several alternatives to counter the deteriorating situation in the Pacific but in the end rejected all of them. The Japanese Minister to Australia suggested a personal visit by Menzies to Tokyo in order to check the drift of the situation, but the memory of Chamberlain's visit to Munich was sufficient to dissuade the Prime Minister from such a venture. Curtin, the leader of the Labour party, at a meeting of the Advisory War Council on August 6 advocated calling a conference which would include the United States, the United Kingdom, the Dominions, and Japan. High Commissioner Bruce in London in turn urged that a warning be given to Japan even though the United States refused to join in the move.[32] At this point, however, Australia was compelled to mark time, for high policy was being formulated in a personal meeting between Churchill and Roosevelt. The day after Bruce dispatched his recommendation to Canberra, the two heads of state began their secret meetings at the Atlantic Conference.

CHAPTER TWELVE

The Pacific War Approaches

W HEN the Atlantic Conference began at Argentia on August 9, the war clouds in the Pacific were rapidly gathering. In less than four months the Pacific war would break out, vastly complicating the problems of prosecuting the war in Europe but resolving the question of American belligerency. It was in an atmosphere of urgency and anxiety that Churchill and Roosevelt sat down at the Atlantic Conference to discuss the war in Europe and the threatening war in the Far East.

The question of policy regarding Japan was the most pressing of the issues discussed at Argentia. Australia was not officially represented at the conference but Australian views received prominent consideration in the conversations. On August 9, the first day of the conference, Sir Alexander Cadogan of the Foreign Office told Welles of the Australian insistence that Churchill obtain from Roosevelt a commitment for military support. Cadogan confided to Welles that Britain had now given the Netherlands East Indies assurance of military support against a Japanese invasion, and Australia wanted the United States to give assurance to the Commonwealth in turn. Specifically, Australia wanted a commitment that

> in the event that Japan attacked the Netherlands East Indies and Great Britain then went to the latter's assistance . . . the President would agree that he would then request of the Congress authority necessary to make it possible for the United States to assist the British, the Dominions and the Netherlands East Indies forces to resist Japanese aggression.

Welles said that the President must rule on the proposal but that he personally opposed such a commitment. If Japan attacked, continued Welles, public opinion in the United States would be the determining influence in any decision reached by the legislature. Welles went on to state his belief that public opinion would support intervention if Japan attacked the Indies and Britain went to her support, and if this estimate were correct any prior commitment would have no practical effect. If a commitment were made, though, and it became known, it would have a bad effect upon American public opinion.[1]

On the evening of the first day of the conference, Churchill proposed to Roosevelt that a joint ultimatum be sent to Japan by the United States, Britain, the Netherlands, the Dominions, and possibly the Soviet Union. The President was, however, thinking in terms of more negotiations with Japan rather than an ultimatum. Shortly before the conference opened at Argentia, the Japanese government had requested the reopening of the Washington conversations, and Roosevelt now told Churchill that he planned to resume the talks if only to gain a moratorium of thirty days. In conferences on August 10 and 11 Churchill abandoned the idea of a joint ultimatum and accepted instead Roosevelt's suggestion for a warning to Japan by the United States. According to Churchill's understanding, the President would inform Nomura that in the event of further Japanese aggression the United States would have to take steps, "notwithstanding the President's realization that the taking of such measures might result in war between the United States and Japan."[2]

On the same day that Roosevelt and Churchill completed the draft of an American warning to Japan (August 11), Menzies cabled Churchill a renewed plea for a strong stand against Japan. He urged that the British countries make it clear to Japan that an attack upon Thailand would be regarded as a *casus belli,* and he recommended that this policy not be made conditional upon American concurrence and active participation. Only if the United States actually objected should the announcement be held up. "We feel," said Menzies, "that if we are prepared to fight America will not in fact desert us."[3] The British, nevertheless, were in no condition to go to the aid of Thailand. This stark reality, together with Roosevelt's desire to pursue time-gaining negotiations, left the Australian proposal stillborn. Churchill apparently believed that the proposed American warning to Japan would be of great help, and he planned to bolster it with British action. A few days after the conference adjourned, the Prime Minister informed Menzies: "President promised me to give the warning to Japan in the terms agreed. Once we know this has been done, we should range ourselves beside him and make clear that if Japan becomes involved in war with United States, she will also be at war with Britain and British Commonwealth."[4]

The warning that Roosevelt gave Japan on August 17 was substantially weaker than Australia desired and even weaker than the one which Churchill and Roosevelt had drafted. Hull considered the injunction which had been agreed upon too strong, and he watered it down before it was delivered. When Roosevelt met with Nomura he stated that if Japan pursued further aggression, the United States would be compelled to take immediately any steps necessary "toward safeguarding the legitimate rights and interests of the United States and American nationals and toward insuring the safety and security of the United States."[5] This did not give Churchill much to range the Commonwealth beside, but he nevertheless framed a supporting statement. In a broadcast on August 24 he said that Britain would take her place by the side of the United States if war came between the United States and Japan.

There is reason to believe that Churchill and his associates were much more satisfied with the results of the Atlantic conference than were Australian leaders. Menzies and his colleagues were intent upon getting a specific commitment from the United States and continued to voice skepticism regarding the likelihood of American military support in a Pacific war. London, on the other hand, knowing the limitations the Constitution and American public opinion imposed upon Roosevelt was more optimistic regarding American support. When in late August the issue of a joint warning to Japan was again raised and again set aside as a result of American representations, London sent to Canberra a clear statement of its expectations of American support:

> You should, however, be aware that the general impression derived by our representative at the Atlantic meeting was that, although the United States could not make any satisfactory declaration on the point, there was no doubt that in practice we could count on United States support if, as a result of Japanese aggression, we became involved in war with Japan.[6]

Meanwhile, the United States had resumed the Washington talks with Japan, but in the subsequent weeks there was virtually not a glimmer of hope for an agreement. The new Japanese proposals which had been presented on August 6 embodied even greater demands than those submitted before the invasion of southern Indochina. Japan demanded that the United States remove its restrictions upon trade, suspend its military measures in the Southwest Pacific area, support Japan in obtaining natural resources from the Netherlands East Indies, and exercise its good offices to bring about direct negotiations between Japan and China. Still implicit was the idea that if China refused to negotiate, the United States would discontinue aid. In return Japan promised to withdraw her troops from Indochina after a settlement had been reached with China, but only on the condition that Japan's "special position" in Indochina, even after the withdrawal, be recognized. The United States, on the other hand, envisaged an agreement along completely different lines. The United States proposed in the succeeding weeks that Japan withdraw completely from China and Indochina. If Japan agreed to this, the United States would restore trade and negotiate on the subject of Manchuria. In other words, the United States would end its economic sanctions and possibly abandon its decade-old policy of nonrecognition *vis-à-vis* Manchukuo if Japan would relinquish all conquests undertaken since 1937.[7]

During September the Washington talks made no headway. Prime Minister Fumimaro Konoye pressed Roosevelt to come to a mid-Pacific conference, but the President refused unless Konoye first submitted promising proposals that would provide the conference with grounds for successful negotiations. This Konoye could not do. If the Prime Minister found Washington rigid, he found his own military colleagues intransigent. War Minister Hideki Tojo demanded that the talks with the United States be dropped and that war commence as soon as Japanese forces were in position. The militarists argued that if they did not fight soon they would not be able to fight with a reasonable hope of victory. Oil and other products would be too scarce. As Tojo later told the International Military Tribunal when on trial, "The elasticity in our national power was on the point of extinction."[8] A decision reached at an Imperial Conference on September 6 gave Konoye's efforts only a brief reprieve. "If by the early part of October there is no reasonable hope of having our demands agreed to in the diplomatic negotiations . . . ," the text of the decision stated, "we will immediately make up our minds to get ready for war against America (and England and Holland)."[9]

The October deadline came and passed with no progress recorded in the Washington talks. Though Ambassador Grew vigorously urged Roosevelt to meet Konoye in Hawaii, Roosevelt and Hull remained convinced that a "meeting of minds" must precede such a conference.[10] Konoye, knowing that the crux of the diplomatic deadlock was the question of Japanese troops in China, pleaded with Tojo to withdraw the troops. When the War Minister rejected his request, Konoye refused to pit himself openly against the Army. Naval leaders, some of whom did not wish to undertake a war with the United States, also refused to take a stand against the Army. As a result, Konoye resigned on October 16 and Tojo was appointed Prime Minister.

In the interim a cabinet change had also taken place in Australia. Since its inception in 1939, the Menzies ministry had been on shaky political ground. The leader of the Country party, Sir Earle Page, had been so indignant when Menzies gained the premiership in 1939 that he had bitterly attacked Menzies and in doing so had split his own party. Arthur W. Fadden broke with Page at that time, and by the end of 1940 had become the new Country party leader. Fadden's emergence facilitated the re-establishment of the Country party-United Australia party coalition, but meanwhile the Labour party had been gaining strength. In the parliamentary elections of September, 1940, Labour won thirty-six seats in the House of Representatives, exactly equivalent to the number occupied by the Menzies-Fadden coalition. The Menzies ministry remained in power only through the support of two independents. During 1941 Labour leaders betrayed an increasing restlessness to topple the non-Labour government. When Menzies suggested in August that he return to London to press the fight for Dominion representation in the United Kingdom War Cabinet, the showdown came. Menzies had announced that he wished to return to London with the consent of the parties, and Labour leaders interpreted this as an artful political dodge, an attempt to gain immunity for his ministry during his absence. The political atmosphere became so turbulent that

Menzies resigned on August 29 and the UAP-UCP coalition chose Fadden as the new Prime Minister.[12] The new ministry was destined to survive little more than a month, for in early October it was to be replaced by a Labour ministry.

During the short Fadden ministry no significant developments occurred in United States-Australian relations. The new Prime Minister welcomed Nelson T. Johnson when he arrived to assume his duties as the United States minister at Canberra, but Johnson had no important issues to take up until the Labour party came to power. The Fadden ministry did, however, witness a significant development in American foreign policy: Roosevelt's "shoot on sight" order. In July the United States had landed forces on Iceland and undertaken the convoying of American, Icelandic, and British ships as far as Iceland. Now on September 11, after an encounter between an American warship and a German submarine, Roosevelt publicly announced that the navy in the Atlantic would protect all merchant vessels and that Axis submarines would be attacked when sighted. In orders to the Atlantic fleet the President even authorized United States warships to escort convoys which included no American ships.[13] Australians warmly applauded the President's move. Prime Minister Fadden declared in the House on September 17 that Roosevelt's speech of September 11 "has inspired us."[14]

The Fadden ministry ended on October 3 when the two independents in the House joined with Labour to defeat the budget. John Curtin, the leader of the Labour party, promptly formed a ministry, the first Labour government in almost a decade. The resurgence of the Labour party was largely attributable to Curtin's capable leadership. When he took over as head of the party upon Scullin's resignation in 1935, he worked diligently and successfully to rid the party of the internal disunity which had sapped its strength ever since the conscription struggle of 1916. Curtin had the personal traits of an effective leader. Though he was somewhat shy and aloof, he possessed a keen mind and a will to succeed. His formal schooling had ended at the age of thirteen, but through self-education as copy boy, labour union official, and politician, he became far more intellectual than the average labour politician. Now as Prime Minister he commanded the respect of his ministerial colleagues and imposed a discipline that no one challenged.

As Minister for External Affairs he chose Herbert V. Evatt, who had left the High Court bench in 1940 to win for Labour a Sydney seat long held by the UAP. Though Evatt had come to the Parliament with such tremendous prestige that he threatened Curtin's position as party leader, the two men now buried their rivalry and worked together effectively. Until Curtin's death in 1945 his top position in the party was never seriously threatened.[15]

The Curtin ministry took office exactly two months before Japan struck at Pearl Harbor on December 7. The ministry thus inherited the tremendous task of preparing for war in the Pacific. The Menzies ministry had accomplished much toward waging war with Britain in the Middle East, but Australia's defensive position in the Far East was woefully weak. Australia had four divisions of the A.I.F. abroad, three in the Middle East and one in Malaya. The Malay Barrier was defended largely by that one Australian division plus two Indian divisions. At home, equipment was so scant that the militia trained without uniforms or rifles. When the Governor General, Lord Gowrie, visited Queensland in 1940, the honor guard at one camp had to stack its rifles hurriedly and send them by truck to another camp where an honor guard was to meet the Governor General a little later.[16]

The new cabinet was in power for only two weeks when the United States presented a request of extraordinary importance: a proposal for the use of Australian air bases by American warplanes. This was the result of a fundamental change in American military plans in the Pacific. In early 1941 the United States had steadfastly resisted British urgings that the Philippines be further reinforced and that the United States plan more than a limited defensive action in the archipelago. But in June, 1941, American policy began to veer to the theory that the Philippines could be held. In late July the Far Eastern Command was created, and General Douglas MacArthur was placed in command of army forces in the Far East. From Manila MacArthur strongly recommended that the attempt be made to hold the Islands in the event of war. At Washington Stimson and other leaders became convinced that bombers might make a decisive difference in defending the area. The B-17 "Flying Fortress" bombers had been so effective in operations from England that it was now believed that they could enable MacArthur to defend the Philippines.[17] In the subsequent weeks the reinforcement of the Islands began in earnest.[18] Then on September 30 the War Department informed MacArthur that it planned to integrate the defense of the Philippines, Australia, the Dutch East Indies, and Singapore by means of improving operating fields throughout the area and augmenting their fuel, bombs, and ammunition. Mac-Arthur was instructed to contact British and Dutch authorities in the Far East regarding establishing airfields at Singapore, Port Darwin, Rabaul, Port Moresby, and Rockhampton. Altogether Mac-Arthur was to be provided with a total air power of 170 heavy bombers, 86 dive bombers, and 195 pursuit planes.[19]

On October 15 the United States dispatched to its envoys in Britain, Australia, New Zealand, and the Netherlands official requests for cooperation in establishing the bases.[20] Minister Nelson Johnson presented the request for the use of Australian air bases to the Australian government on October 17. Australian bases at Rabaul, Port Moresby, Darwin, and Rockhampton were designated as those desired for training and familiarization of American personnel and for the storage of supplies.[21] The use of these bases was required particularly as part of a new Hawaiian-Philippine route, for strategists anticipated that in the event of war the direct route through Guam could not be held.[22] It was proposed that the bases be constructed or improved by the Australian government with the United States giving financial and technical assistance.[23]

The Australian government readily agreed to furnish the bases, and Johnson was assured that Australia wished to give the "fullest cooperation possible."[24] Australian leaders were doubtless aware that the request for use of bases was a major step in the direction of American intervention in event of a Japanese attack on British possessions. The request seemed further to confirm Churchill's general impression at the Atlantic conference that in practice the Commonwealth could count on United States support in a war with Japan. In reality, however, the bases project had little military significance until after the outbreak of war, for no work was done on them before December 7. Plans had been drawn up, nevertheless, and the project eventually involved an expenditure of £5,684,000 in Australia.[25]

Tokyo soon learned that important negotiations were underway between the United States and Australia. The newspapers in Sydney and Melbourne printed stories about negotiations for a united front among the United States, Australia, New Zealand, the Netherlands Indies, Britain, and China; and these news reports doubtless resulted from a leak to the press from the Australian government. Some of the stories even referred to communications sent to the Australian government by the United States. Hull was considerably perturbed that the Australian government allowed secret information to seep to the press,[26] but the Department of State recognized that the results were not all bad. One official at the Department observed that the stories may have produced "a not unfavorable effect both in Australia and abroad."[27]

Several developments at this time probably caused concern in Tokyo. In September Australia opened direct diplomatic relations with China, sending Sir Frederic Eggleston as minister to Chungking.[28] Still more significant was Britain's move to strengthen Singapore. Australia had long pleaded with the United Kingdom government to send capital ships to the East, and late in October Churchill cabled Curtin that the *Prince of Wales* was going to join the *Repulse* in the Indian Ocean, and as soon as they were ready, the four "R" battleships (the *Resolution, Ramillies, Revenge,* and *Royal Sovereign*) would be moved to Eastern waters.[29]

A guarded optimism prevailed among the ABD (American-British-Dutch) powers during September and October while measures were being initiated to strengthen their military posture in the Far East, but the optimism was shortlived. Early in November alarm over Japanese troops in Indochina revived. This time there was anxiety about a possible Japanese offensive into Yunnan, China, from northern Indochina. The apprehension began when Chiang Kai-shek appealed to Churchill for British air units from Singapore to reinforce the Chinese Air Force and the American Volunteer Group.[30] The British Prime Minister was sufficiently concerned to revive the proposal for a joint Anglo-American warning to Japan.

Churchill took the initiative for a joint warning when he forwarded Chiang's appeal to Roosevelt on November 5. He told the President that Britain was willing to make some pilots and aircraft available to the Chinese. He then tackled the larger issue of a joint warning. "What we need now is a deterrent of the most general and formidable character." The policy of gaining time which the President had championed at Argentia had been "brilliantly successful," he said, "But our joint embargo is steadily forcing the

Japanese to decisions for peace or war." He hoped that the United States would now warn Japan, and if this could be done, Britain would do likewise.[31]

In Washington the proposal for a joint warning was debated for several days but in the end again rejected. Though some officials at the State Department favored the project, Hull and others continued to object to a warning unless it could be reinforced by military force. The Joint Board of the Army and Navy canvassed the whole issue on November 5 and in a lengthy memorandum to the President agreed with Hull's position.[32] Two days later Roosevelt told Churchill that continuing efforts to strengthen defenses in the Philippines and at Singapore would increase Japan's hesitation but that a formalized verbal warning might have an opposite effect. Thus the project for a joint warning collapsed once more. There was, nevertheless, a significant by-product of the episode of which London and Canberra were unaware. In the course of the deliberations over the warning proposal, American military thinking with regard to the Far East crystallized as it had not done before. The Joint Board's memorandum to the President of November 5 stated that military action against Japan should be undertaken if Japan attacked the territories of the British Commonwealth or the Netherlands East Indies or if Japanese forces moved into Thailand west of the hundredth meridian, or into Thailand's Kra Isthmus south of the tenth parallel, or into Portuguese Timor, New Caledonia, or the Loyalty Islands.[33]

With the United States' rejection of the joint warning, Australia evidenced considerable impatience with the American attitude and with Britain's policy of deferring to American diplomatic leadership in the Pacific. Australia pressured London to take a resolute line with Japan and to give a warning to Japan even if American participation could not be secured. British action, Curtin cabled on November 8, should not be delayed merely on account of American hesitancy. Four days later Sir Earle Page, who had been sent to London to present the Australian point of view, told Churchill and other British leaders that the United Kingdom should not adhere to its insistence that the United States always retain the lead *vis-à-vis* Japan. A more resolute stand by Britain, he thought, would force the United States to recognize the necessity of coming to her aid. To this Churchill answered that though Britain should maintain a stiff attitude toward Japan, she should not become involved in war unless there was assurance of American participation.[34] Churchill obviously felt that American intervention would best be achieved by allowing Washington to hold the initiative in dealing with Japan. The Prime Minister accepted Page's contention, however, that the Empire would be obliged to act even if the United States refrained, but he pointed out that the longer Britain could delay action, the greater would be the chance of American participation. Churchill went on to caution Page that it would be a great error to push Roosevelt to act in advance of American opinion. He said that when Roosevelt was pressed too hard, "a sudden wall of silence would descend on proceedings for several weeks."[35]

While the whole issue of United States-Australian-United Kingdom relations was being surveyed in London, Japan was making crucial decisions which would resolve the question of American intervention in no uncertain way. On November 5 the Japanese Privy Council, meeting in the presence of the Emperor, set the first deadline on the Washington conversations at "about November 25." The next day operational orders were issued for the attacks against American as well as British and Dutch positions (shortly set for December 8, Japanese time). Also on this same November 5 Nomura was notified of the approval of Japan's final proposals, and he was ordered to submit them at Washington. He was further informed that Sabura Kurusu was being sent to Washington by Trans-Pacific Clipper to assist in the final talks. Events were now picking up momentum and were racing toward a showdown.

CHAPTER THIRTEEN

Eleventh-Hour Diplomacy

THE final Japanese proposals were formulated in two groups: Plan A and Plan B. Plan A was a comprehensive proposal for an overall settlement. Its provisions require no extensive analysis, for Australia was to have no part in the deliberations over this set of terms. On the crucial issue of evacuation of troops from China, the plan fell far short of what the United States had insisted upon throughout the conversations. The Japanese troops were to remain in North China and the Mongolian border regions for a "suitable period," while the troops in other areas would be evacuated in two years. To Nomura Tokyo explained that "suitable period" meant about twenty-five years. The troops in Indochina were to remain until a just peace was established or the China Incident was successfully concluded.[1]

The Japanese knew when they presented Plan A to Hull on November 7 that it was unlikely to be accepted, thus they had drawn up Plan B as a final stopgap proposal. The Japanese terms for a *modus vivendi* were not submitted until after Kurusu's arrival on November 15, and in the interim the United States and the British Commonwealth were drawing more closely together. On November 7 the Roosevelt administration virtually decided that the United States would aid the Commonwealth if Japan struck southward. When Roosevelt polled his cabinet on that day, its members agreed unanimously that the American people would support such a move.[2] Two days later Churchill announced that should the United States become involved in war with Japan, the British declaration would "follow within the hour."[3]

Kurusu arrived in Washington on November 15 and saw Roosevelt and Hull two days later. He discerned immediately that the

Japanese proposals of Plan A and the yet-to-be-presented Plan B would not break the deadlock, and on November 18 he suggested to Hull a limited agreement involving a return to the status quo of July. This proposal, calling for Japanese evacuation of southern Indochina and American cancellation of its freezing order, was communicated by Hull to Casey, as well as to the British and Dutch representatives,[4] but the plan, it soon developed, was not acceptable to Tokyo.[5] Consideration now switched to Plan B which Kurusu and Nomura presented to Hull on November 20.

Until the Japanese offered Plan B, Australia and the other members of the Commonwealth had virtually no part in the Washington conversations. Now, less than three weeks before the outbreak of war, Australia was invited to join the active consultations. At this point, however, the United States and Japan were as far from an agreement as they had been when the conversations began months before, and Plan B did not close the gap. By its terms the United States would be required to stop all aid to China, cancel the freezing order, supply Japan with a required quantity of oil, and help Japan secure products from the Netherlands Indies. In return for these concessions—concessions which would virtually assure China's collapse—Japan would promise not to make any armed advance in southeastern Asia and the southern Pacific. The troops in Indochina were to be withdrawn only after peace between Japan and China was restored or an equitable peace in the Pacific area was established.[6] As these terms were discussed with Commonwealth representatives, Hull knew that the time for consideration was short. Army and Navy cipher experts had broken the Japanese code, and Hull knew the text of messages from Tokyo to Nomura and Kurusu. One of those messages had set the deadline on November 25. Shortly before this deadline was to expire the critical date was moved up to November 29, but the Tokyo message had a note of finality: "After that things are automatically going to happen."[7]

Hull's first meeting with the Commonwealth, Dutch, and Chinese representatives took place on November 22. Hull briefed Casey and the others on the Japanese-American conversations and concluded with the Japanese proposal for a *modus vivendi*. "There seemed to be general agreement," Hull noted, "that a substitute was more desirable than a specific reply to the Japanese proposal, section for section." Hull and his associates at the Department had already been drafting a counter-proposal, and he outlined the draft reply to those present. Hull found that Casey, Halifax, and the Dutch Minister, Dr. A. Loudon, were well pleased with the report. The Chinese Minister, Dr. Hu Shih, was "somewhat disturbed," an indication of difficulties to come.[8]

Hull met again with the ABCD representatives on November 24 and presented them with a definite draft for an American reply. The text of the *modus vivendi* included the following:

1. Both powers would undertake not to make by force or threat of force any advancement across any international border in the Pacific area.
2. Japan would withdraw from southern Indochina and limit forces in northern Indochina to 25,000.
3. Both powers would remove their freezing restrictions, but exports from each country would remain subject to the respective export control measures which each country may have in effect for reasons of national defense.
4. The United States would approach the British and Dutch governments with a view to those governments removing their freezing restrictions on the same basis.
5. The United States would not look with disfavor upon the opening of Sino-Japanese negotiations for a peaceful settlement of their differences.
6. The *modus vivendi* would remain in effect for no longer than three months unless renewed by common agreement.[9]

The discussion of the *modus vivendi* at the meeting was long but, from Hull's point of view, unsatisfactory. Casey and the other representatives apparently had waited for this definite draft before sounding their governments, while Hull expected them already to have contacted their governments on the basis of the conference of two days before. It was an unfortunate but natural misunderstanding. Hull, with fuller sources of information, was more conscious of the time limitations. Also, after months of exasperating negotiations with the Japanese, his patience was wearing thin. When he found that only the Netherlands minister had heard from his government, he told Casey and the others that he was definitely disappointed at the "lack of interest and lack of a disposition to cooperate." Hull closed the session with the remark that he was not sure that he would present the proposals to the Japanese without knowing anything about the views of their governments.[10]

Hull interpreted the November 24 conference as an indication of lack of support for the *modus vivendi* proposal. His conclusion that the Australian government was indifferent or cool to the project was certainly not justified. On the contrary, Casey cabled his government on the same day of this meeting urging that an effort be made to get an agreement. He felt that the Japanese proposals were unacceptable but that with modification an agreement might be reached. In Australia the Minister for External Affairs, Evatt, agreed that the Japanese proposals should not be rejected outright and that everything possible should be done to avoid a breakdown of the talks. In a telegram to Casey on November 26, Evatt completely backed the proposal to relax the economic restrictions against Japan in return for a Japanese withdrawal in Indochina, provided Japan gave a general guarantee not to advance elsewhere.[11]

Though the Australian government supported the *modus vivendi* project, it was poorly informed about the status of the Washington negotiations and the intentions of the Japanese. In his cables to Casey, Evatt spoke of "opportunities for considerable discussions, amendments, counter-proposals," while those in Washington knew that the deadline was fast approaching. Evatt also believed that the Japanese were clearly "anxious to avoid war" and he criticized the "rigid" American attitude which he thought was driving Japan toward a war of desperation.[12] Washington and London were in large part responsible for the meager information available in Australia, but a further factor was the inaccurate reports coming from the Australian legation in Tokyo. Chargé Keith Officer, the former Australian liaison officer at Washington, cabled his government on November 22 that the Japanese government wished to avoid at present anything that might prejudice discussions in Washington. A week later on the very day that the Japanese deadline expired (November 29), Officer cabled that the balance of opinion was that the government would allow some time for further consideration of terms.[13]

Evatt's belief that the "rigid" American attitude was forcing Japan to war was soon proved wrong. It was not American "rigidity" but rather the position of the British government, particularly its support of China, which gave the *coup de grâce* to the *modus vivendi* project. No sooner had Hull presented the proposals to the ABCD powers than the blows began raining down upon the whole effort. Halifax told Hull on November 25 that his government believed the United States should pitch its demands high and its price low. London suggested that the United States stipulate not only the total withdrawal of Japanese troops but also of naval and air forces from Indochina and the prohibition of further military advances against China or any other region. Hull replied that it would be utterly impractical to request such stiff terms,[14] but in the subsequent days the British government continued to balk at Hull's milder proposals.

Heavier blows soon fell. Chiang Kai-shek instructed his minister at Washington to oppose the project, and he also sent a protest to Churchill. By the evening of November 25 the future of the *modus vivendi* was already in doubt, and late that night at 12:55 A.M. a cable reached Washington which sealed its fate. Churchill, in a personal message, reminded Roosevelt of the basic dilemma that had haunted American policy since the beginning of the Washington conversations:

> Of course, it is for you to handle this business and we certainly do not want an additional war. There is only one point that disquiets us. What about Chiang Kai-shek? Is he not having a very thin diet? Our anxiety is about China. If they collapse, our joint dangers would enormously increase. We are sure that the regard of the United States for the Chinese will govern your action. We feel that the Japanese are most unsure of themselves.[15]

This message, together with reports that Japanese troops were already embarked and moving south, convinced Hull that the *modus vivendi* proposal should be dropped.

On November 26 Hull, with Roosevelt's approval, gave to the Japanese a reply which in effect ended the talking stage. The Ten Point American program which Hull presented incorporated the maximum demands which the United States had made during the long negotiations.[16] This reply, issued without any consultation with other governments or even the United States War Department, obviously was designed to keep the record straight rather than to serve as a basis for negotiations. When Secretary of War Stimson inquired on November 27 what had been done, Hull replied: "I have washed my hands of it and it is now in the hands of you and Knox—the Army and the Navy."[17]

Australia struggled vigorously but vainly to save the *modus vivendi* project from collapse. Casey saw Hull on November 27 and when Hull told him that the *modus vivendi* was permanently abandoned, he expressed great concern. The Secretary told Casey that he did not consider that the communications from Churchill and Eden would be very helpful in a bitter fight that would be stirred up by China. In other words, if the Roosevelt administration were going to make proposals which might leave it open to charges of appeasement, the administration must have the support of the British government before proceeding. When Casey inquired whether it would be feasible to take the matter up further with the Chinese, Hull replied that he did not think so.[18] The Australian government did, nevertheless, immediately raise the question with the Chinese government. As a result of a suggestion by Menzies in the Advisory War Council, the government instructed Minister Eggleston to urge China to withdraw its opposition. The Australian attitude toward China at this time was well summed up in words ascribed to Curtin: "China does not want to be treated as a pawn in this game, but neither does Australia."[19]

In Washington Casey also did everything he could to save the talks from collapse. After talking with Evatt by telephone on November 29, he proposed to Hull that Australia offer herself to Japan as mediator between the United States and Japan. Hull said frankly that the diplomatic stage was over and that nothing would come of such a move,[20] but Casey nevertheless went ahead with the idea. He visited Kurusu at the Japanese Embassy on the morning of the thirtieth and offered to pass on to Hull any proposal the Japanese might have to offer. Kurusu had no proposal to make, however, other than that discussions should be taken up again on the Japanese outline for a *modus vivendi*. The following day (December 1) Prime Minister Curtin was still hoping that something could be salvaged from the situation. In a minute of the War Cabinet he noted:

> We again repeat our opinion that, even at this late stage, a further endeavour should be made to encourage the United States to establish a *modus vivendi* with Japan which can be made satisfactory to China as well as to the other powers concerned.[21]

The Australian initiative was doomed from the outset, for Hull had rung down the curtain on negotiations with the Ten Point Program on November 26. Hull's actions in these last days before the outbreak of war probably will be the source of historical controversy for many years. Through the maze of controversy that has already developed, one fact stands out clearly. It was exceedingly questionable for the American Secretary of State to seal the fate of the Japanese-American conversations, as he did on November 26, without prior consultation with the British, the Dominions, and the Dutch on the Ten Point Program. Unquestionably the chances of agreement were small indeed. Hull had estimated the chances at the outset of the conversations at one in a hundred, and by November 26 the chances were perhaps one in a thousand. It was unfortunate, nevertheless, that Hull discarded that one chance in a thousand before consultation with the other interested governments.[22]

As the war approached, Australian leaders had one question uppermost on their minds: would the lead given by the United States in talking be followed by a similar lead in armed defense against Japan? In a cable to London on November 29, Prime Minister Curtin inquired what Britain would do either in the absence of United States armed support or with the assistance of the United States. To this question Britain gave no precise answer. On November 30, however, Australia was informed that an attempt would be made to clarify the American position. In a cable from the Dominions Office, Australia was told that Japan appeared to be poised to attack Thailand's Kra Isthmus, just north of Malaya, and that the British Ambassador at Washington had been instructed to ask Roosevelt for his views regarding British action to forestall the Japanese.[23] The importance of this inquiry at Washington was not appreciated in Australia, perhaps because of the vagueness of the message from the Dominions Office. Actually, Britain was contemplating the occupation of the Kra Isthmus in order to anticipate a Japanese invasion of the area and was asking Roosevelt for a specific commitment of armed support if war resulted from such action.[24]

Before Halifax reported the results of his soundings at Washington, Australia evidenced considerable impatience with Britain's policy of deferring to American leadership. On December 1 the Australian War Cabinet advised London to take a stand regardless of American support. Australia recommended that the Far East commander, Sir Robert Brooke-Popham, be given authority to move troops into the Kra Isthmus if reconnaissance established that a

Japanese force were approaching the area. This should be done with or without the cooperation of the United States, though the United States should be asked whether it had any objection. The next day Curtin cabled London that in case of a Japanese attack on Thailand, Britain should not lend armed support without assurance of active cooperation by the United States, but that if Japan threatened to move into the Kra Isthmus, British action to occupy the area should not depend upon American support. He also urged that the Netherlands East Indies be assured of armed support regardless of the American attitude.[25]

At London, Prime Minister Churchill made it clear to Australia's representatives that he was not willing to set out upon a course independent of the United States. When on December 1 he conferred with Sir Earle Page and Stanley M. Bruce, he told them that the British policy was to "march in line with the United States of America." If Japan attacked British territory, Britain would immediately declare war on Japan but otherwise would wait for America.[26] Churchill stated that this attitude had been adopted on global-political grounds rather than on those of local strategic lines. He conceded, however, that the position would be reviewed in the next few days. He had made personal representations to America and expected an early reply.[27]

Information soon arrived from Washington which resolved the Anglo-Australian differences. Halifax reported a conference with Roosevelt on December 1 at which the President promised support in the Pacific. If Japan attacked the Dutch or the British, the President had told Halifax, "we should obviously all be together." Two days later Halifax conferred with Roosevelt again and received further clarification of the American position. Roosevelt stated that when he talked of giving support to the British and the Dutch he meant "armed support." The commitment also would apply if Japan attacked Thailand and Britain went to her aid. Roosevelt said he agreed with Britain's plans for operations in the Kra Isthmus if Japan attacked Thailand and that Britain could count on American backing, though in this latter contingency support might not be forthcoming for a few days.[28]

On December 5 Australia and the other Dominions received from London the welcome news that the long-sought assurance from the United States had at last been given. The telegram to Canberra stated that a commitment of armed support had been received and that it covered the following: (a) if Britain found it necessary either to forestall a Japanese landing in the Kra Isthmus or to occupy part of the Isthmus as a counter to the Japanese violation of any other part of Thailand; (b) if the Japanese attacked the Netherlands East Indies and Britain at once went to the support of the Netherlands; (c) if the Japanese attacked British territory. The message went on to say that Brooke-Popham at Singapore had been authorized to order the move into the Kra Isthmus without reference to Whitehall if reconnaissance established the fact that escorted Japanese ships were approaching the Isthmus or if the Japanese violated any other part of Thailand. Brooke-Popham had also been instructed to put into effect the plans agreed to with the Dutch if the Japanese attacked the Netherlands East Indies.[29]

Several aspects of Roosevelt's assurance to Britain are obscure. Whether the assurance covered a prior British move into Thai territory is debatable. Roosevelt told Halifax that he approved of Britain's plans regarding the Kra Isthmus *if Japan attacked Thailand.* In practice it would have been difficult to judge which side was taking prior action. Britain planned to occupy the Isthmus only if Japan violated Thai territory or if a Japanese expedition were sighted approaching the Isthmus. It is likely that Roosevelt's commitment was sufficiently comprehensive to cover this latter contingency, though it is doubtful that it would have covered a British move prior to the sighting of such an expedition. Actually, the issue would not have arisen, even if Japan had not attacked American territory. When the moment of decision arrived, the British feared the Japanese might be deliberately maneuvering them into taking prior action. The result was that the plan for occupation of the Kra Isthmus was never ordered into operation.[30]

Another aspect of Roosevelt's assurance which remains uncertain is whether the President intended to order American armed forces into action without a congressional declaration of war. The fact that Roosevelt and his cabinet members spent the last days before the outbreak of war drafting a message to the Congress strongly indicates that he intended to present the question of peace or war to the Congress. Roosevelt and his entire cabinet were convinced that the American public would support intervention to aid Britain.[31] It is likely, therefore, that his commitment was based upon his conviction that the Congress would immediately issue a declaration of war rather than upon an intention to bypass the Congress.[32]

Australian leaders were, of course, elated at the news of Roosevelt's assurance of armed support. Throughout 1941 Australia had constantly sought such a commitment from Washington. Now that it had been made, Australia wished to use it as a deterrent. On December 6 Casey conferred with the President and urged the issuance of a joint warning to Japan. The proposed draft stated that if Japan attempted to establish her influence in Thailand by force or threat of force, she would do so "at her own peril." Roosevelt was at that time considering sending an appeal to the Japanese Emperor, and he therefore ruled out such a warning, at least until the effect of his message to the Emperor could be appraised. Casey was told by the President that he desired to wait until the evening of December 8 for a reply from the Emperor and that if no reply were forthcoming by that time he would then issue a warning to Tokyo in the form of a message to the Congress and the American people on December 9. The warnings by the British and others could follow on December 10.[33] When the results of Casey's interview were known in London and Canberra, it was agreed that they would defer to the wishes of the President.

In the last hours before the Japanese attack, the United States continued to hold the initiative among the ABD powers. In London and Canberra—though somewhat less so in the latter—leaders were content to let Roosevelt keep the leadership. The most important of all Anglo-Australian objectives at this juncture was to secure American intervention, and if Roosevelt believed this could be achieved more readily by the United States retaining the initiative, the ABD powers were willing to go far in acceding to the President's leadership. Thus the President's schedule was followed. The British and Dutch withheld their warnings, and Roosevelt's message to the Emperor was dispatched to Tokyo on the evening of December 6. The move had no effect upon the course of events; on December 1 the Japanese had already made the final decision for war.[34] The day after the sending of the message, Britain, Australia, and the United States found themselves no longer wrestling with diplomatic proposals but fighting as allies against the formidable military forces of Japan.

CHAPTER FOURTEEN

Conclusions

THE outbreak of the Pacific War allied Australia and the United States in the common struggle against Japanese hegemony in Asia and German hegemony in Europe. On January 1, 1942, that alliance was accorded formal recognition when Australia and the United States, along with twenty-four other nations, signed the Declaration of United Nations. By that declaration the signatories pledged themselves to make no separate peace and to use their full economic and military resources to defeat the members of the Tripartite Pact. Henceforth, both in war and in peace, the United States and Australia would be tied together by the bonds of common objectives and mutual dependence.

The ten years preceding the alliance had been a decade fraught with conflicting policies and divergent attitudes, a period in which enmity yielded to a friendship dictated by powerful forces outside both the United States and Australia. The decisive influences cementing the interests of the two countries were Japan's march to empire in the Far East and Britain's compelling need for a rapprochement *en grande* with the United States due to the rise of Hitler in Europe.

Throughout the decade the United States and Australia were slow to perceive their common interests and their need for mutual cooperation and friendship. In matters of trade there was little foundation for friendship, since both sides were limited by circumstances that could not be easily changed. Nevertheless, much irritation might have been avoided by a more skillful handling of the trade issue by both Washington and Canberra. On the Australian side the trade diversion program, viewed with the perspective of history, appears almost incomprehensible. However much provocation Australia had received, the decision in 1936 to wage a trade war against Japan, her only conceivable enemy in the Far East, and the United States, the most powerful nation on the Pacific, was about as improvident as any decision could be. The timing could hardly have been more unfortunate. The year 1936 saw Japan's shattering of naval limitation and Germany's tearing up of the Versailles Treaty. These events, as well as other fractures in the structure of world security, caused Britain to seek a rapprochement with the United States at the same time Australia was moving in the opposite direction. The result was that Australia stumbled into an untenable position from which she extricated herself only after a period of painful readjustment and political embarrassment. The whole episode might have been avoided if Australia had consulted with London before acting. Australia often complained to London— and with much justice—regarding lack of consultation with the Dominions, but in this instance Empire consultation broke down on the Australian side, with melancholy results.

Whether the United States might have treated Australia more favorably in matters of trade is open to question. During the 1930's a pall of hopelessness regarding Australian trade hung over official Washington. James C. Dunn provided a deep insight into the Department of State's attitude when he wrote to Consul General Moffat in 1936 that "we do not know exactly how we could ever give even a measure of satisfaction to the Australians through the negotiation of a trade agreement."[1] The unhappy fact that Australia exported items which were produced in the United States—many of them in surplus quantities—limited what the Roosevelt administration could do. Secretary of Agriculture Wallace admitted on occasion that a lower offer on the wool tariff could have been made in negotiations in 1938-1939 if merely economic factors had been taken into consideration. Nevertheless, both Wallace and Hull felt that the political aspects of the question could not be ignored. Hull was convinced that to do so would jeopardize the entire reciprocal trade program. Whether Hull's fears were entirely justified may be debated. The records of the Department leave no doubt that those fears were genuine and were not put forward just as an excuse. Domestic political concerns, however, can provide a justification only for the executive branch of the government and not for the United States as a nation. If Wallace's estimate regarding the economic aspects were correct, the United States could have offered Australia during the trade talks a lower rate than was proposed on the crucial wool tariff.

There was one area of negotiations in which Washington could have adopted a more liberal attitude without incurring any political risks. Entry and residence rights could have been granted to Australian businessmen. With a four- or six-to-one favorable balance of trade, the United States could have well afforded to extend such rights without raising extraneous issues in order to get a *quid pro quo*. There is no reason to believe that the Australian government would have regarded such a concession as of great value, for it would have done little to redress the unfavorable balance of trade. The granting of such a concession would nevertheless have mitigated in some small measure Australia's resentment.

The refusal of the United States to grant entry and residence rights was due largely to resentment in American official circles over British imperial preference, a resentment heightened in 1932 by Britain's adoption of the Ottawa program. To American officials Empire preference was an unadulterated evil. Washington never thought through the full implications of its attitude toward the preferential system. British advocates of Empire preference of a later day have pointed out rather effectively the inconsistency of American policy in the controversy between multilateralism and preferential systems.[2] In the post-World-War-II era, the United States encouraged a common market on the continent of Europe while continuing to push its multilateral program in opposition to the Commonwealth's imperial preference. Doubtless political and strategic considerations—the desire to create a strong Europe—dictated United States policy toward the common market. But such considerations might also have justified a more tolerant view of imperial preference in the 1930's. The preferential system was the economic foundation of the British Commonwealth and the economic prosperity and strength of the Commonwealth was of vital interest to the United States.

That the existence of the Commonwealth of Nations was politically and strategically valuable to the United States was only dimly appreciated in Washington. The thinking of the Roosevelt administration, which was more favorably inclined toward Britain than was the general public, tended to center upon British imperialism and was not overly generous in its appraisal. If the memoirs of Ambassador Halifax supply an accurate index, Roosevelt gave more thought to how Hong Kong could be returned to China than to the contribution Britain was making to political stability in South Asia, Southeast Asia, and the Southwest Pacific.[3] It is only necessary to view that area of the world a generation later to appreciate the vital role the British Empire and Commonwealth was filling. By the 1960's the United States had been obliged to move in and take over the accumulated problems of French colonial misrule, the former Dutch colony lay in a state of economic and political chaos, while the former British colonies, with the sole exception of Burma, stood as monuments to Britain's stabilizing political influence. If Washington had taken a wider view of its own interests in the 1930's it would have set a higher value upon the Empire and Commonwealth and would have viewed its economic system, if not with beneficence, at least with a larger measure of equanimity.

Fortunately, the resentment among American officials over imperial preference and Australian trade discriminations did not filter down to the American public. The Department of State gave the press sparse information, and the American public remained uninformed and largely uninterested in the issues of United States-Australian relations. Even during the trade diversion program the American public exhibited little reaction. In Australia public opinion was of more consequence, but even there the public was largely uninformed. The Australian government handed to the press only information of a vague and general character. Even the newspapers in Sydney and Melbourne, which were in closest touch with governmental circles, abounded in "press rumors" but little solid information. The Australian public had enough information, however, to sustain its resentment against the United States until world events compelled a change in attitudes. If more information had been released to the public, it is not likely that it would have brought much change in Australian sentiments, though Australian officials asserted at times that it would have increased resentment. Ironically, the American public was so disinterested in Australian affairs that it was not even aware that Australians disliked them. Australian enmity, so far as the American public was concerned, remained unknown and unrequited.

With the approach of war in Europe in 1939, Australian hostility toward the United States began to evaporate rapidly. The economic disputes which caused so much acrimony were almost totally eclipsed by the crucial issues of security and survival. From the outbreak of the Second World War in September, 1939, to December, 1941, the overriding concern was whether the United States would aid Britain in Europe and Australia in the Pacific. As the Pacific War approached, Australia became more and more desperate to obtain a commitment for armed support from the United States.

Throughout the endeavor to secure a commitment from the United States, Australia evidenced scant understanding of the difficult constitutional position that Roosevelt was in. The Constitution in unequivocal terms lodged war-making power in the Congress. Roosevelt could not incur a commitment that would bind the Congress, nor could he make any categorical threats of war against Japan when the Congress might not back up such threats. Roosevelt finally made a commitment on December 1 and 3, when he became convinced that Congress and public opinion would sustain that pledge, but even at that late date he could not absolutely guarantee its fulfillment—unless he committed forces to battle without a congressional declaration of war, and it is highly unlikely that he had such an intention. Sumner Welles gave the clearest explanation of the problem when he told Sir Alexander Cadogan at the Atlantic conference that public opinion would be the determining factor in any decision reached by the legislature, that he believed the public would support war if Japan attacked Britain, but that if a prior commitment were made and became known, it would have a bad effect upon American public opinion.[4]

Ambassador Halifax well understood the constitutional problem faced by Roosevelt. Thus Sumner Welles could record his remarks to Halifax in August, 1941: "I said that Lord Halifax was fully familiar with our constitutional system and that consequently no definite commitments or threats to this effect could officially be made."[5] The memoirs of Halifax also substantiate the ambassador's understanding of the American Constitution.[6] Churchill likewise comprehended Roosevelt's position. He often sought a commitment from the President and urged the sending of a joint warning to Japan, but he never evidenced the impatience with Roosevelt's "constitutional difficulties" that Australian leaders felt. On several occasions he cautioned the Australian government against pushing Roosevelt too far ahead of American public opinion. Australian leaders, and even some Americans, believed that Roosevelt might have moved faster than he did toward intervention, but Lord Halifax did not agree. Looking back upon these events many years later, Halifax said of Roosevelt: "His judgment of what American public opinion would stand at any particular moment was seldom far astray."[7]

Throughout most of 1941—certainly from August, 1941 on—London remained confident that if and when the final crisis came in the Pacific, United States armed support could be counted upon. Churchill was therefore content to allow the United States to retain the diplomatic leadership in dealing with Japan. Neither Menzies, Curtin, Evatt, nor Casey had the same abiding faith in Roosevelt that Churchill possessed, hence their constant preoccupation with the endeavor to win a firm commitment from Washington. Typical of the Australian attitude was Menzies' plea to London on July 30, 1941: "If the Americans feel in their hearts that in the event of warlike retaliation [to sanctions] by Japan they could not remain aloof from the conflict, surely they can be made to see that a plain indication by them to Japan at this stage would probably avoid war."[8] However logical this reasoning appeared to Australian leaders, it could not be reconciled with the United States Constitution. Moreover, later events showed that Australia (and the United Kingdom) overrated the deterrent power of a threat to Japan by the United States. Japan assumed that the United States would intervene and made her plans accordingly. Right up to December, 1941, Australia exhibited distrust of American diplomatic leadership and questioned Churchill's policy of deferring to that leadership. Not until news arrived on December 5 of Roosevelt's firm commitment were Australian anxieties finally dispelled.

The coming of the Pacific war and the forging of the wartime alliance between the United States and Australia did not solve all the contentious problems in their relations. Nor did it mean that the closest possible friendship had yet been achieved. The two countries had, nevertheless, moved a long way toward that goal while traveling the road from enmity to alliance. Throughout that journey the most helpful influence had undoubtedly been that of the British home government. At every crucial turn of the road the

United Kingdom had given decisive direction. In the Matson shipping dispute, the trade diversion issue, and finally in the diplomacy preceding the Japanese onslaught, London had employed its influence to compose differences and to foster understanding between the United States and Australia. In the future years with the spread of American power across the Pacific and the attainment by Australia of a full sense of nationhood, the role of the United Kingdom in United States-Australian relations was to decline in importance. But whatever regret the British may have felt when the United States assumed a position of first importance in Australian strategic conceptions, they could justifiedly pride themselves upon their contribution toward building friendship between the two Pacific nations.

Notes

Chapter One

1. Melbourne *Herald,* December 27, 1941.
2. Australian Institute of International Affairs, *Australia and the Pacific,* Princeton, 1944, p. 11.
3. Australian Institute of International Affairs, *Australia and the Pacific,* p. 3. An excellent discussion of Australian attitudes toward the mother country and Australian nationalism is given in W. K. Hancock, *Australia,* New York, 1930, pp. 54-68.
4. Canberra Study Group, "Australia's Interests in the Pacific Basin," in *Australia and the Pacific* (Australian Supplementary Papers: British Commonwealth Relations Conference, 1938), p. 10. Of total Australian exports in 1937-1938 the United Kingdom took: butter, ninety-two per cent; beef, ninety-nine per cent; mutton and lamb, ninety-eight per cent; wool, thirty-seven per cent. Giselle Schneider, "The Australian Tariff," in G. L. Wood, editor, *Australia: Its Resources and Development,* New York, 1954, p. 227.
5. Tredwell to Henry L. Stimson, September 8, 1931, File 847.00/154, Department of State Records, National Archives, Washington, D.C.
6. Moffat diary, October 3, 1935, Nancy Harvison Hooker, editor, *The Moffat Papers: Selections from the Diplomatic Journals of Jay Pierrepont Moffat, 1919-1943,* Cambridge, 1956, pp. 128-31.
7. Doyle to Stimson, June 8, 1932, File 847.00/168.
8. United States Tariff Commission, *An Analysis of the Trade Between Australia and the United States,* Prepared in response to Senate Resolution 334, 72nd. Congress, 2nd. Session, February, 1934.
9. L. Lawrence and G. H. Palmer, "The Economic Consequences of Ottawa in the Pacific Dominions," Documents of the Fifth Conference of the Institute of Pacific Relations, 1933, VIII, 12-13.
10. W. S. Kelley, "The Australian Tariff," in *Australian Economic Policies* (Australian Supplementary Papers: British Commonwealth Relations Conference, 1938), pp. 16-18; Members of the Canberra Branch, Australian Institute of International Affairs, "Australia's Commercial Policy in Relation to Article VII of the Mutual Aid Agreement Between the United States and the United Kingdom," in *Australia and the Pacific,* Princeton, 1944, pp. 186-87.
11. Statistics are from United States Tariff Commission, *An Analysis of the Trade Between Australia and the United States.*
12. Cotton to John D. Hickerson and J. Theodore Marriner, January 12, 1930, File 711.415 Traders/6. During the negotiations the United

States offered to grant entry and residence rights if Australia would not include in tariff assessments the inland freight charges incurred in the sending country. In order to keep tariff assessments as low as possible, manufacturers in the Eastern part of the United States had adopted the practice of sending goods across the continent by way of Canadian railroads. This brought complaints to the United States government from the railroad companies in the United States which lost business to the Canadian lines. Australia was unwilling to agree to this because the concession would have to be extended to all countries and would thus result in considerable loss of revenue. The records of the negotiations are found in State Department Files 711.472 and 711.415 Traders. Many of the documents are published in United States, Department of State, *Papers Relating to the Foreign Relations of the United States, 1927*, 3 vols., Washington, 1942, I, 437-41; *Papers Relating to the Foreign Relations of the United States, 1931*, 3 vols., Washington, 1946, I, 839-43; and *Foreign Relations of the United States: Diplomatic Papers, 1934*, 5 vols., Washington, 1950-1952, I, 831-44.

13. Tredwell to Stimson, September 8, 1931, File 847.00/154.

14. Memorandum by John R. Minter, Division of Western European Affairs, October 28, 1936, File 811.71247H/69; Memorandum by Jesse E. Saugstad, Division of Trade Agreements, February 17, 1936, File 811.71247H/59.

15. Consul General John K. Caldwell to Stimson, October 12, 1932, File 847.00/174.

16. Memorandum by Minter, February 24, 1936, United States, Department of State, *Foreign Relations of the United States: Diplomatic Papers, 1936*, 5 vols., Washington, 1953-1954, I, 708-10.

17. On the cruiser controversy see Robert H. Ferrell, *American Diplomacy in the Great Depression: Hoover-Stimson Foreign Policy, 1929-1933*, New Haven, 1957, ch. vi.

18. E. A. Ferguson, T. P. Fry, J. G. Holmes, and A. Murray Smith, "Australian Foreign Policy—Formation and Expression of Australian Opinion," in *Australian Policies, Political and Strategic* (Australian Supplementary Papers: British Commonwealth Relations Conference, 1938), p. 3. An Australian view of the crisis is given in Frederick Morley Cutlack, *The Manchurian Arena: An Australian View of the Far Eastern Conflict*, Sydney, 1934.

19. William Macmahon Ball, editor, *Press, Radio and World Affairs, Australia's Outlook*, Melbourne, 1938, pp. 44-46.

20. Stimson's policy is analyzed in Ferrell, *American Diplomacy in the Great Depression*, chs. viii-xi; Richard N. Current, *Secretary Stimson: A Study in Statecraft*, New Brunswick, 1954, chs. iv-v; Sara R. Smith, *The Manchurian Crisis, 1931-1932: A Tragedy in International Relations*, New York, 1948. British policy is discussed in R. Bassett, *Democracy and Foreign Policy: A Case History, The Sino-Japanese Dispute, 1931-33*, London, 1952.

21. Eugene H. Dooman to Maxwell M. Hamilton and Stanley K. Hornbeck, January 21, 1935, File 847.00/212.
22. Moffat to Secretary of State Cordell Hull, October 12, 1935, File 747.94/17.
23. Moffat diary, October 3, 1935, *The Moffat Papers,* pp. 128-31.
24. Moffat to Hull, February 11, 1936, File 747.94/20.

Chapter Two

1. Caldwell to Hull, telegram, June 5, 1934, *Foreign Relations, 1934,* I, 841-42; Caldwell to Hull, June 7, 1934, File 611.4731/98.
2. Memorandum by John D. Hickerson, June 6, 1934, File 611.4731/93.
3. O'Brien to the Department of State, August 10, 1934, *Foreign Relations, 1934,* I, 843-44.
4. Cordell Hull, *The Memoirs of Cordell Hull,* 2 vols., New York, 1948, I, 352-77.
5. Hull to Caldwell, January 15, 1935, United States, Department of State, *Foreign Relations of the United States: Diplomatic Papers, 1935,* 4 vols., Washington, 1952-1953, II, 9-10.
6. Caldwell to Hull, February 8, 1935, *Foreign Relations, 1935,* II, 10-13.
7. Minter to Hull, April 8, 1941, File 611.4731/429.
8. Lyons might have taken back to Australia something more than expressions of good will if he had reopened the issue of entry and residence rights. Before Lyons arrived, Hull wrote to Roosevelt saying that if Lyons opened the subject the Department was now willing to go forward with the treaty on entry and residence. Lyons did not, however, bring up the subject. Hull to Roosevelt, July 5, 1935, File 611.4731/28A.
9. Moffat to Grew, January 27, 1935, Moffat Papers, Houghton Library, Harvard University, Cambridge, Massachusetts.
10. Moffat diary, October 3, 1935, *The Moffat Papers,* pp. 128-31.
11. Moffat to Hull, October 14, 1935, File 611.4731/137.
12. Moffat diary, October 5, 1935, Moffat Papers.
13. Moffat to Hull, telegram, March 4, 1936, *Foreign Relations, 1936,* I, 742-43.
14. Hull to Moffat, telegram, March 6, 1936, *Foreign Relations, 1936,* I, 743.
15. Moffat to Hull, telegram, March 16, 1936, *Foreign Relations, 1936,* I, 743-44; Moffat to Hull, March 16, 1936, File 611.4731/146.
16. Australia, *Commonwealth Parliamentary Debates,* 14th. Parliament, 1st. Session, vol. 149, p. 759. Gullett's speech on that day summarizing efforts to secure a trade treaty with the United States is given in D. B. Copland and C. V. Janes, editors, *Australian Trade Policy: A Book of Documents, 1932-1937,* Sydney, 1937, pp. 238-41.

146 · *Notes*

17. Moffat to Hull, telegram, April 6, 1936, *Foreign Relations, 1936,* I, 745-46.

18. Hull to Lyons, telegram, April 10, 1936, *Foreign Relations, 1936,* I, 746-47.

19. Moffat to Hull, April 28, 1936, File 611.4731/159.

20. Australia, *Commonwealth Parliamentary Debates,* 14th. Parliament, 1st. Session, Vol. 150, p. 1489.

21. Moffat diary, May 20, 1936, Moffat Papers.

22. Moffat to Hull, May 22, 1936, *Foreign Relations, 1936,* I, 751-52. The new tariff duties were to go into effect immediately, though they had to be validated by Parliament within six months in order not to lapse. In December, 1936, the necessary parliamentary approval was given.

23. Moffat to Hull, telegram, May 23, 1936, *Foreign Relations, 1936,* I, 752-53.

24. Moffat to Hull, telegram, June 5, 1936, *Foreign Relations, 1936,* I, 756.

25. Moffat to Hull, May 25, 1936, File 647.116/165.

26. Moffat diary, June 1, 1936, *The Moffat Papers,* pp. 132-37. Hull's protest is in Hull to Moffat, telegram, May 27, 1936, *Foreign Relations, 1936,* I, 753-54.

27. Pearce to Moffat, June 6, 1936, *Foreign Relations, 1936,* I, 757-60.

28. Hull to Moffat, June 29, 1936, File 611.473/22a.

29. Moffat to Hull, June 3, 1936, File 647.003/323.

30. Press reaction is given in Ball, *Press, Radio and World Affairs,* pp. 39-41. Other criticisms of trade diversion are given in Copland and Janes, editors, *Australian Trade Policy,* pp. 299-324.

31. Jack Shepherd, *Australia's Interests and Policies in the Far East,* New York, 1940, pp. 25-26.

32. Shepherd, *Australia's Interests and Policies in the Far East,* pp. 27-42. The restrictions on Japanese imports are analyzed in *The Economic Record: The Journal of the Economic Society of Australia and New Zealand,* Melbourne, 1925-, XII, 276-81.

33. Public exchanges between Lyons and Japanese spokesmen are given in Copland and Janes, editors, *Australian Trade Policy,* pp. 264-84.

34. Shepherd, *Australia's Interests and Policies in the Far East,* pp. 59-62; F. Eric Hitchins, *Tangled Skeins: A Historic Survey of Australian Wool Marketing,* Melbourne, 1956, pp. 58-60.

35. The agreement, which was to run for eighteen months, gave Japanese piece goods a quota eighteen per cent below the level of imports in 1935. Australian wool was given a quota by Japan which was twenty-nine per cent below the level of the same year. Moffat to Hull, telegram, December 28, 1936, File 647.9431/46. During July to December, 1936, while the trade war with Japan was underway, Aus-

tralian exports to Japan were little more than £500,000 compared with over £8,000,000 in the same period of 1935. Japanese exports to Australia in the same period dropped only from £3,300,000 to £3,100,000. *The Round Table*, London, 1910-, No. 107 (June, 1937), pp. 658-60.

36. Minter to Moffat, May 28, 1936, Moffat Papers. In an editorial on May 28 the New York *Times* opposed retaliatory action, pointing out that the United States would probably lose more than would Australia if such a policy were followed.

37. Memorandum by Hull, August 26, 1936, *Foreign Relations, 1936,* I, 766-67.

38. Moffat to Hull, May 25, 1936, File 647.116/165.

39. Moffat to Norman H. Davis, June 19, 1936, Moffat Papers.

40. Moffat diary, November 3-4, 1936, Moffat Papers.

41. Moffat diary, February 11-12, 27-28, 1937, Moffat Papers.

42. Sir Earle Page, *Truant Surgeon: The Inside Story of Forty Years of Australian Political Life,* Sydney, 1963, p. 246.

43. Dunn to Moffat, October 1, 1936, Moffat Papers.

44. Minter to Moffat, July 4, 1936, Moffat Papers.

45. Hull to Bingham, October 16, 1936, *Foreign Relations, 1936,* I, 770-71.

46. Moffat diary, January 25, 1937, *The Moffat Papers,* p. 143.

47. Moffat to Hull, February 3, 1937, File 611.4731/208.

48. Moffat diary, March 10, 1937, *The Moffat Papers,* p. 144. The London *Times* correspondent in Canberra agreed. He cabled London on March 12, "It is believed that one result of the resignation will be a general review of the trade diversion policy, particularly against the United States."

49. Moffat to Hull, February 15, 1937, United States, Department of State, *Foreign Relations of the United States: Diplomatic Papers, 1937,* 5 vols., Washington, 1954, II, 137-38.

Chapter Three

1. Moffat to Hull, October 26, 1936, *Foreign Relations, 1936,* I, 711-14.

2. Consul General George A. Bucklin to Hull, October 26, 1936, File 811.71247H/66; Moffat to Hull, October 26, 1936, *Foreign Relations, 1936,* I, 711-14.

3. Memorandum by Minter, October 28, 1936, File 811.71247H/69.

4. Memoranda by Hull, October 28 and November 3, 1936, *Foreign Relations, 1936,* I, 714-15, 715-16.

5. Moffat to Hull, October 26, 1936, *Foreign Relations, 1936,* I, 711-14.

6. Moffat to Hull, December 19, 1936, File 811.71247H/72.

7. Shortly before leaving Australia, Moffat completed a long and tedious series of negotiations for the importation of American aircraft

into Australia. Since 1928 an Australian customs regulation had prohibited the importation of aircraft from countries not signatory to the International Convention for the Regulation of Aerial Navigation, thus banning American aircraft. In the negotiations the United States attempted to get a general agreement for reciprocal recognition of airworthiness certificates, but Australia insisted upon an import licensing system, probably to protect British interests in the Australian market. Moffat convinced Washington that *any* arrangement for importation of American aircraft would be a significant victory, and a licensing system was agreed upon in early 1937. *Foreign Relations, 1936*, I, 774-82.

8. Australia, Department for External Affairs, *Report, 1936*, Canberra, 1936, pp. 8-10; Richard G. Casey, *The Conduct of Australian Foreign Policy*, Brisbane, 1952, pp. 14-15. The growing Australian interest in external affairs was also evidenced in 1936 by the beginning of the publication of *Current Notes on International Affairs* by the Department for External Affairs.

9. Moffat diary, November 3-4, 1936, Moffat Papers.

10. Moffat to Hull, January 4, 1937, File 847.00/247.

11. Australia, Eastern Mission, *The Australian Eastern Mission, 1934* (Report of the Right Hon. J. G. Latham, Leader of the Mission), Canberra, 1934.

12. Australia, Department for External Affairs, *Report, 1936*, p. 87, and *Report, 1937*, p. 73.

13. E. A. Ferguson, T. P. Fry, J. G. Holmes, and A. Murray Smith, "Australian Foreign Policy—Formation and Expression of Australian Opinion," *Australian Policies, Political and Strategic* (Australian Supplementary Papers: British Commonwealth Relations Conference, 1938), pp. 3-4; Canberra Study Group, "Australia's Interests in the Pacific Basin," p. 5.

14. Paul Hasluck, *The Government and the People, 1939-1941*, Canberra, 1952, pp. 69-70.

15. Bingham to Hull, telegram, June 4, 1937, File 033.4711Lyons/ 38.

16. Grew to Hull, telegram, May 28, 1937, File 700.0011Pacific/ 15.

17. Memorandum by Hornbeck, June 4, 1937, File 033.4711Lyons/ 38.

18. Memorandum by Hornbeck, June 8, 1937, File 700.0011Pacific/ 27.

19. Memorandum by Hornbeck, June 30, 1937, File 700.0011Pacific/22.

20. Atherton to Hull, June 17, 1937, File 700.0011Pacific/18.

21. Bingham to Hull, telegram, June 4, 1937, File 033.4711Lyons/ 38.

22. An analysis of press reaction is given in Ball, *Press, Radio and World Affairs*, pp. 51-53.

23. British embassy to the Department of State, June 16, 1937, *Foreign Relations, 1937*, II, 95-98.

24. Kennedy to Hull, July 1, 1937, *Foreign Relations, 1937*, II, 98-103.

25. Memorandum by Moffat, August 9, 1937, *Foreign Relations, 1937*, II, 106.

Chapter Four

1. Minter to Moffat, June 16, 1937, Moffat Papers.
2. Squire to Moffat, May 25, 1937. Moffat Papers.
3. Doyle to Moffat, May 27, 1937, Moffat Papers.
4. Bingham to Hull, June 4, 1937, *Foreign Relations, 1937*, II, 141-42.
5. Minter to Moffat, June 19, 1937, Moffat Papers.
6. Minter to Hickerson, July 8, 1937, Moffat Papers.
7. Hull to Bingham, telegram, June 10, 1937, *Foreign Relations, 1937*, II, 142-43.
8. Memorandum by Dunn, July 1, 1937, *Foreign Relations, 1937*, II, 144-50.
9. Minter to Moffat, June 26, 1937, Moffat Papers.
10. Minter to Hickerson, July 8, 1937, Moffat Papers.
11. Moffat to Squire, August 14, 1937, Moffat Papers.
12. Moffat diary, September 18, 1937, Moffat Papers.
13. Memorandum by Moffat, October 8, 1937, File 611.4731/242.
14. Doyle to Hull, November 10, 1937, File 847.00/269.
15. Doyle to Moffat, November 25, 1937, Moffat Papers.
16. British embassy to Department of State, December 9, 1937, *Foreign Relations, 1937*, II, 151-52.
17. Wilson to Hull, December 10, 1937, File 647.116/314.
18. Memorandum by Moffat, January 11, 1938, United States, Department of State, *Foreign Relations of the United States: Diplomatic Papers, 1938*, 5 vols., Washington, 1954-1956, II, 121-23.
19. Memorandum by Hickerson (Assistant Chief of the Division of European Affairs), December 10, 1937, *Foreign Relations, 1937*, II, 153-54; Moffat diary, December 18, 1937, Moffat Papers.
20. Wilson to Hull, December 10, 1937, File 647.116/314.
21. Wilson to Hull, December 23, 1937, *Foreign Relations, 1937*, II, 157-59.
22. Wilson to Hull, telegram, December 23, 1937, *Foreign Relations, 1937*, II, 157-59.
23. Memorandum by Minter, December 28, 1937, File 611.4731/251 1/2.
24. Hull to Wilson, telegram, January 10, 1938, *Foreign Relations, 1938*, II, 120-21.
25. Memorandum by Moffat, January 14, 1938, *Foreign Relations, 1938*, II, 123-24.

26. Wilson to Hull, telegram, January 15, 1938, *Foreign Relations, 1938,* II, 124-26.

27. Memorandum by Moffat, January 19, 1938, *Foreign Relations, 1938,* II, 126-28.

28. Receipts of farmers in the United States had risen to 9.2 billion dollars in 1937, compared to 5.4 billion in 1933. In those same years the index of farm prices (August, 1909-July, 1914=100) had risen from 70 to 122. Murry R. Benedict, *Farm Policies of the United States, 1790-1950,* New York, 1953, p. 314.

29. Memorandum by Moffat, January 19, 1938, *Foreign Relations, 1938,* II, 126-28.

30. Memorandum by Moffat, January 22, 1938, *Foreign Relations, 1938,* II, 128-29; British Embassy to Department of State, January 22, 1938, *Foreign Relations, 1938,* II, 129-30.

31. Hickerson to Sayre, January 24, 1938, File 611.4731/276.

32. Hull to Wilson, January 25, 1938, *Foreign Relations, 1938,* II, 130-31.

33. *Parliamentary Debates,* 15th. Parliament, 1st. Session, Vol. 155, p. 390.

34. Quoted in Hartley Grattan, editor, *Australia,* Berkeley, 1947, p. 137.

35. Keith Feiling, *The Life of Neville Chamberlain,* London, 1946, p. 308.

36. W. G. K. Duncan, editor, *Australia's Foreign Policy,* Sydney, 1938, see especially pp. 94-96, 195.

Chapter Five

1. Moffat diary, January 6, 1938, Moffat Papers.

2. Moffat to Wilson, January 29, 1938, Moffat Papers.

3. Department for External Affairs, *Report, 1936,* pp. 91-94; *Report, 1938,* pp. 96-97; C. A. S. Hawker, "Australia's Foreign Trade Treaties," *Australian Economic Policies* (Australian Supplementary Papers: British Commonwealth Relations Conference, 1938), pp. 3-8; Copland and Janes, editors, *Australian Trade Policy,* pp. 200-14, 242-44, 251-57.

4. Moffat to Wilson, January 29, 1938, Moffat Papers.

5. Moffat diary, January 4, 1938, Moffat Papers.

6. Moffat to Wilson, January 6, 1938, Moffat Papers.

7. Johnson (London) to Hull, telegram, January 1, 1938, File 847.415/27.

8. Hull to Johnson, telegram, January 7, 1938, File 847.415/27; Hull to Wilson, telegram, January 12, 1938, File 847.415/33.

9. Wilson to Hull, February 15, 1938, File 847.415/51; Wilson to Hull, June 30, 1938, File 847.415/55.

10. Memorandum by Henry L. Deimel, Jr., Assistant Chief of the Division of Commercial Treaties and Agreements, February 4, 1938,

Foreign Relations, 1938, II, 133-34; Memorandum by John R. Minter, Division of European Affairs, February 17, 1938, *Foreign Relations, 1938,* II, 136-37; Memorandum by John H. Fuqua, Division of Commercial Treaties and Agreements, March 3, 1938, *Foreign Relations, 1938,* II, 137-38; Memorandum by Harry C. Hawkins, Chief of the Division of Commercial Treaties and Agreements, March 11, 1938, *Foreign Relations, 1938,* II, 139-40.

11. List of Australian requests, February 4, 1938, File 611.4731/ 298; List of United States requests, February 17, 1938, File 611.4731/ 289B.

12. Memorandum by Fuqua, February 10, 1938, *Foreign Relations, 1938,* II, 134-35.

13. Memorandum by Hawkins, March 11, 1938, *Foreign Relations, 1938,* II, 139-40.

14. Moffat diary, March 10, 1938, Moffat Papers.

15. Memorandum by Fuqua, February 10, 1938, *Foreign Relations, 1938,* II, 134-35.

16. Memorandum by Hawkins, March 11, 1938, *Foreign Relations, 1938,* II, 139-40.

17. Memorandum by Hawkins, March 11, 1938, *Foreign Relations, 1938,* II, 141.

18. Memorandum by Minter, April 20, 1938, *Foreign Relations, 1938,* II, 145-48.

19. Memorandum by Minter, June 4, 1938, File 611.4731/329. Those present were Sayre, Moffat, Hickerson, Minter, Fuqua, and Muccio.

20. Memorandum by Sayre, June 11, 1938, File 611.4731/344.

21. Department of State to the British embassy, June 13, 1938, *Foreign Relations, 1938,* II, 149-50.

22. List of possible concessions and requests handed to the British ambassador, June 13, 1938, File 611.4731/331A.

23. Moffat diary, June 13, 1938, Moffat Papers.

24. Memorandum by Moffat, June 23, 1938, File 611.4731/327.

25. British embassy to the Department of State, June 28, 1938, *Foreign Relations, 1938,* II, 150-51.

26. Department of State to the British embassy, June 29, 1938, *Foreign Relations, 1938,* II, 151-52.

27. Memorandum by Hawkins, July 6, 1938, File 611.4731/335.

28. Memorandum by Hawkins, July 6, 1938, File 611.4731/335.

29. Minter to Moffat, July 8, 1938, Moffat Papers; Moffat to Wilson, July 29, 1938, Moffat Papers.

30. Memorandum by Moffat, August 12, 1938, *Foreign Relations, 1938,* II, 152-54.

31. Moffat to Wilson, October 12, 1938, Moffat Papers.

32. Department for External Affairs, *Report, 1938,* p. 99.

33. Wilson to Hull, telegram, November 19, 1938, *Foreign Relations, 1938,* II, 155-56.

34. British embassy to the Department of State, December 10, 1938, *Foreign Relations, 1938,* II, 159-60.

35. Memorandum by Fuqua, December 10, 1938, *Foreign Relations, 1938,* II, 157-58.

36. Memorandum by Fuqua, December 7, 1938, File 611.4731/370.

37. Moffat diary, December 17, 1938, Moffat Papers.

38. New York *Times,* January 3, 1939.

39. Moffat diary, December 17, 1938, Moffat Papers.

40. Memorandum by Minter, January 10, 1939, United States, Department of State, *Foreign Relations of the United States: Diplomatic Papers, 1939,* 5 vols., Washington, 1955-1957, II, 325-27.

41. Memorandum by Herbert Feis, February 17, 1939, File 611.4731/398.

42. Memorandum by Minter, June 29, 1939, *Foreign Relations, 1939,* II, 328-29.

43. Moffat to Wilson, June 16, 1939, Moffat Papers.

44. In the Geneva negotiations after World War II the United States offered and Australia accepted a twenty-five per cent reduction on wool. This meant a tariff rate reduced from thirty-four cents down to twenty-five cents per pound on fine wool. The tariff, in terms of *ad valorem* equivalent, was reduced still further by inflation. The postwar negotiations are discussed extensively in D. F. Nicholson, *Australia's Trade Relations: An Outline History of Australia's Overseas Trading Arrangements,* Melbourne, 1955.

Chapter Six

1. Hull, *Memoirs,* I, 576-77.

2. Wilson to Hull, April 5, 1938, File 847.00/275.

3. Hasluck, *The Government and the People,* pp. 40-42; P. F. Irvine, "The Defense of Australia," *Australian Policies, Political and Strategic* (Australian Supplementary Papers: British Commonwealth Relations Conference, 1938), p. 11.

4. Hasluck, *The Government and the People,* p. 99.

5. Hull, *Memoirs,* I, 579-80.

6. Quoted in Nicholas Mansergh, *Survey of British Commonwealth Affairs: Problems of External Policy, 1931-1939,* London, 1952, p. 167.

7. The terms and significance of the Anglo-Italian agreement are discussed in P. A. M. van der Esch, *Prelude to War: The International Repercussions of the Spanish Civil War (1936-1939),* The Hague, 1951, pp. 139-55. The controversy over policy toward Italy is analyzed in Winston S. Churchill, *The Gathering Storm,* Boston, 1948, pp. 239-58; Randolph S. Churchill, *The Rise and Fall of Sir Anthony Eden,* London, 1959, pp. 124-50; and Feiling, *Life of Neville Chamberlain,* pp. 334-39.

8. Hull, *Memoirs,* I, 581-82.

9. Shepherd, *Australia's Interests and Policies in the Far East,* pp. 80-87, 156-58; Don Whitington, *The House Will Divide: A Review of*

Australian Federal Politics in the Past Twenty Five Years, Melbourne, 1954, p. 51. In May, 1938, the ministry announced that the exportation of iron ore would be prohibited after July 1, but this action was based upon the needs of national defense.

10. Shepherd, *Australia's Interests and Policies in the Far East,* p. 158. It provided for substantially the same quotas as the previous agreement of December, 1936.

11. Hull, *Memoirs,* I, 587.

12. Langer and Gleason, *Challenge to Isolation,* p. 40.

13. Sydney *Morning Herald,* August 22, 1938.

14. Hasluck, *The Government and the People,* pp. 94-95. Feiling, the sympathetic biographer of Chamberlain, states that Chamberlain's reluctance to go to war during the Czechoslovakian crisis was due in part to the attitude of the Dominions. *Feiling, Life of Neville Chamberlain,* p. 362.

15. Hull, *Memoirs,* I, 591-94; Langer and Gleason, *Challenge to Isolation,* pp. 32-35.

16. Count Ciano's diary indicates that Mussolini's intervention was due primarily to the British appeal rather than to that of Roosevelt. Andreas Mayor, translator, *Ciano's Hidden Diary, 1937-1938,* New York, 1953, pp. 165-66.

17. Hasluck, *The Government and the People,* p. 95.

18. Wilson to Hull, December 1, 1938, File 847.00/287.

19. Langer and Gleason, *Challenge to Isolation,* pp. 46-48.

20. Wilson to Hull, December 1, 1938, File 847.00/287; Wilson to Hull, January 7, 1939, File 847.00/289.

21. Wilson to Hull, May 2, 1939, File 847.00/302; Melbourne *Herald,* April 15, 1939.

22. Hasluck, *The Government and the People,* pp. 109-15. Writing of Menzies in 1951, Sir George Pearce said: "Possessed of a mordant and at times devastating gift of humour, he is held in high respect by his political opponents. He has the advantage of a trained legal mind combined with a natural aptitude for clarity of expression. He suffered somewhat from the habit of sometimes hitting critics with unnecessary force, thus leaving a tinge of bitter resentment in the mind of the recipient of his verbal thrusts. This arises largely from the quickness of his own powers of perception and a rather obvious impatience with those of slower wit. Longer experience in the Federal arena has greatly modified this trait."—Sir George F. Pearce, *Carpenter to Cabinet: Thirty-Seven Years of Parliament,* London, 1951, p. 193.

23. Quoted in Hasluck, *The Government and the People,* p. 118.

24. Memorandum by Moffat, December 23, 1938, File 124.47/6.

25. Memorandum by Moffat, May 4, 1939, File 701.4711/39.

26. Wilson to Hull, telegram, May 11, 1939, File 124.47/8; Wilson to Hull, May 15, 1939, File 847.00.301.

27. Wilson to Hull, December 1, 1938, File 847.00/287.

28. Wilson to Hull, July 3, 1939, File 847.00/304.

Chapter Seven

1. Hasluck, *The Government and the People,* pp. 149-52.
2. Wilson to Hull, telegram, September 8, 1939, File 847.248/30.
3. Hull, *Memoirs,* I, 692; Moffat to Wilson, September 30, 1939, Moffat Papers.
4. Wilson to Hull, October 2, 1939, File 847.00/307.
5. Wilson to Hull, November 1, 1939, File 847.00/308.
6. Lothian to Hull, November 27, 1939, *Foreign Relations, 1939,* II, 329.
7. Hull to Roosevelt, December 16, 1939, File 701.4711/60. The New York *Times* said on February 21, 1940, "Australia has given her best in sending us Richard G. Casey. The London *Times* expressed similar views on January 11, 1940. Don Whitington in *The House Will Divide,* pp. 68-72, speculates that Casey had been chosen by Lyons as his successor and that Menzies sent him to Washington in order to be rid of a political rival. However, Sir Earle Page, who was in the middle of the political struggle, gives no support to this conjecture in his detailed account in *Truant Surgeon,* pp. 262-89.
8. Doyle to Hull, May 14, 1941, File 647.116/381. Australia's overseas reserves had dropped in September, 1939, to their lowest point since 1931. The yearly adverse balance of payments reached its lowest point of £A30,700,000 in 1940-41. After that the United States expenditures in Australia reversed the trend. By June 30, 1945, Australia had overseas reserves of £A208,300,000. J. C. Horsfall, *Australia,* New York, 1955, pp. 192-93.
9. Memorandum by Hull, June 6, 1940, File 740.0011EW1939/3870.
10. Hull, *Memoirs,* I, 788.
11. Menzies to Roosevelt, telegrams, May 26 and June 14, 1940, File 841.248/499; Roosevelt to Menzies, telegrams, May 31 and June 20, 1940, File 841.248/464 and 482.
12. United States, Department of State, *Foreign Relations of the United States: Diplomatic Papers, 1940,* 5 vols., Washington, 1955-61, IV, 13-14.
13. United States, Department of State, *Papers Relating to the Foreign Relations of the United States: Japan, 1931-1941,* 2 vols., Washington, 1943, II, 285: Langer and Gleason, *Challenge to Isolation,* p. 589.
14. Memorandum by Under Secretary of State Sumner Welles, May 16, 1940, *Foreign Relations, 1940,* IV, 20-21; Herbert Feis, *The Road to Pearl Harbor,* Princeton, 1950, pp. 51-57.
15. Hull, *Memoirs,* I, 896; Feis, *Road to Pearl Harbor,* p. 66.
16. Memorandum by Hornbeck, June 26, 1940, *Foreign Relations 1940,* IV, 362-64.
17. British embassy to the Department of State, June 27, 1940,

Foreign Relations, 1940, IV, 365-67; Memorandum by Hull, June 27, 1940, *Foreign Relations, 1940,* IV, 367.

18. Memorandum by Hull, June 28, 1940, *Foreign Relations, 1940,* IV, 369; Hull to Lothian and Casey, June 28, 1940, *Foreign Relations, 1940,* IV, 370-72; Hull, *Memoirs,* I, 896-99.

19. Hasluck, *The Government and the People,* p. 226.

20. Frederick L. W. Wood, *The New Zealand People at War: Political and External Affairs* (Official History of New Zealand in the Second World War), Wellington, 1958, p. 197.

21. J. R. M. Butler, *Grand Strategy: Volume II, September 1939-June 1941* (History of the Second World War), London, 1957, pp. 328-29.

22. Sir Llewellyn Woodward, *British Foreign Policy in the Second World War* (History of the Second World War), London, 1962, p. 166.

23. Wood, *The New Zealand People at War,* p. 198.

24. Woodward, *British Foreign Policy in the Second World War,* p. 167.

25. Hull, *Memoirs,* I, 900-01.

26. Langer and Gleason, *Challenge to Isolation,* pp. 721-23.

27. William L. Langer and S. Everett Gleason, *The Undeclared War, 1940-1941,* New York, 1953, pp. 6-7, 17-18.

28. Joseph C. Grew, *Ten Years in Japan,* New York, 1944, *passim;* Joseph C. Grew, *Turbulent Era: A Diplomatic Record of Forty Years, 1904-1945,* 2 vols., Boston, 1952, *passim.*

29. John Morton Blum, *From the Morgenthau Diaries,* Boston, 1959, pp. 485-92; Harold L. Ickes, *The Secret Diary of Harold L. Ickes,* 3 vols., New York, 1953-1954, III, 273-74.

30. Stimson and Bundy, *On Active Service,* pp. 311-12, 382-85; Feis, *Road to Pearl Harbor,* pp. 49-50.

31. Feis, Road to Pearl Harbor, pp. 88-93; Current, *Secretary Stimson,* pp. 144-46.

32. Hasluck, *The Government and the People,* p. 525 .

33. Langer and Gleason, *Undeclared War,* pp. 9-15; Feis, *Road to Pearl Harbor,* pp. 96-98.

34. Memorandum by Hull, September 16, 1940, *Foreign Relations, 1940,* IV, 120-21; Hull, *Memoirs,* I, 906.

35. Memorandum by Berle, September 27, 1940, *Foreign Relations, 1940,* IV, 156-57.

36. Hasluck, *The Government and the People,* p. 227; Lionel Wigmore, *The Japanese Thrust* (Series I, no. IV, *Australia in the War of 1939-1945*), Canberra, 1957, p. 25.

37. Memorandum by Berle, September 3, 1940, File 893.154/297½.

38. Feis, *Road to Pearl Harbor,* pp. 101-09.

39. Quoted in Langer and Gleason, *Undeclared War,* p. 21.

40. Text of the pact is given in *Foreign Relations: Japan, 1931-1941,*

II, 165-66. The pact is analyzed in Feis, *Road to Pearl Harbor,* pp. 110-21; Robert J. C. Butow, *Tojo and the Coming of the War,* Princeton, 1961, pp. 160-87; Paul W. Schroeder, *The Axis Alliance and Japanese-American Relations,* 1941, Ithaca, 1958, *passim;* Frank W. Ikle, *German-Japanese Relations, 1936-1940,* New York, 1956, *passim.*

41. Memorandum by Hull, September 30, 1940, *Foreign Relations, 1940,* IV, 159-60; Hull, *Memoirs,* I, 911.

42. Lothian to Lady Astor, October 7, 1940, quoted in J. R. M. Butler, *Lord Lothian (Philip Kerr),* London, 1960, p. 303.

43. Memorandum by Berle, September 27, 1940, *Foreign Relations, 1940,* IV, 156-57.

Chapter Eight

1. Langer and Gleason, *Undeclared War,* p. 38.

2. Winston S. Churchill, *Their Finest Hour,* Boston, 1949, pp. 497-98.

3. Langer and Gleason, *Undeclared War,* p. 40.

4. Elting E. Morison, *Turmoil and Tradition: A Study of the Life and Times of Henry L. Stimson,* Boston, 1960, p. 522.

5. United States, Congress, *Pearl Harbor Attack: Hearings of the Joint Committee on the Investigation of the Pearl Harbor Attack,* 39 vols., Washington, 1945-1946, I, 264-66.

6. Langer and Gleason, *Undeclared War,* p. 43.

7. Memorandum by Hull, November 12, 1940, *Foreign Relations, 1940,* IV, 206-07.

8. Memorandum by Berle, November 15, 1940, *Foreign Relations, 1940,* IV, 212-13.

9. Memorandum by Hull, November 25, 1940, *Foreign Relations, 1940,* IV, 220-21; Hull, *Memoirs,* I, 914.

10. Memorandum by Hull, September 16, 1940, *Foreign Relations, 1940,* IV, 120-21.

11. Memorandum by Hull, September 30, 1940, *Foreign Relations, 1940,* IV, 159-60.

12. Churchill, *Their Finest Hour,* pp. 497-98.

13. Memorandum by Hull, October 5, 1940, *Foreign Relations, 1940,* IV, 167-68.

14. Memorandum by Hull, October 7, 1940, *Foreign Relations, 1940,* 168-69.

15. Memorandum by Hornbeck, October 21, 1940, *Foreign Relations, 9410,* IV, 188-89; Memorandum by Hornbeck, October 30, 1940, *Foreign Relations,* 1940, IV, 198.

16. Hasluck, *The Government and the People,* pp. 294-97; Major General S. Woodburn Kirby, *The War Against Japan* (History of the Second World War), 3 vols. to date, London, 1957-, I, 49-50; Wigmore, *The Japanese Thrust,* pp. 40-45.

17. Memorandum by Hull, October 16, 1940, *Foreign Relations, 1940,* IV, 184; Memorandum by Berle, October 21, 1940, File 701.4711/85.

18. Memorandum by Welles, December 10, 1940, *Foreign Relations, 1940,* IV, 231-32.

19. The Australian representatives were Rear-Admiral M. W. S. Boucher, Major-General J. Northcott, and Air Vice-Marshal S. J. Groble.

20. Langer and Gleason, *Undeclared War,* pp. 285-87; Mark S. Watson, *Chief of Staff: Prewar Plans and Preparations* (United States Army in World War II), Washington, 1950, pp. 369-78; Maurice Matlof and Edwin M. Snell, *Strategic Planning for Coalition Warfare, 1941-1942* (United States Army in World War II), Washington, 1953, pp. 34-38.

21. Samuel Eliot Morison, *History of United States Naval Operations in World War II: The Rising Sun in the Pacific,* Boston, 1948, p. 50.

22. *Pearl Harbor Attack,* XV, 1485-1550.

23. Langer and Gleason, *Undeclared War,* pp. 287-88.

24. Casey to Hull, February 17, 1941, Hull Papers, Library of Congress, Washington, D.C.

Chapter Nine

1. Minter to Hickerson, Dunn, Moffat and Stewart, July 19, 1940, Moffat Papers.

2. Gauss to Hull, August 10, 1940, File 124.47/27.

3. Gauss to Hull, November 5, 1940, File 124.47/30.

4. Gauss to Moffat, November 12, 1940, Moffat Papers.

5. Gauss to Hull, October 1, 1940, File 701.4794/17.

6. Gauss to Moffat, November 12, 1940, Moffat Papers.

7. Gauss to Hull, September 17, 1940, File 847.00/318.

8. Gauss to Hull, November 18, 1940, File 847.00/322.

9. C. Hartley Grattan, "An Australian-American Axis?" *Harper's Magazine,* CLXXX (December-May, 1939-1940), 561-69.

10. Fred Alexander, "Australia and the United States," *The Australian Quarterly,* XIII (No. 1, March, 1941), 5-13.

11. C. Hartley Grattan, "Australia and the Pacific Stalemate," *Asia,* XLI (1941), 169-71. See also Grattan, "Australia through Australian Eyes," *Asia,* XLI (1941), 613-17. Grattan stated the problem concisely: "Their solid information about the United States was limited and they were not in a good position to interpret the information that reached them." Grattan, *The United States and the Southwest Pacific,* Cambridge, 1961, p. 156.

12. *The Round Table,* CXXIII (June, 1941).

13. Canberra Looks Abroad," *The Austral-Asiatic Bulletin,* III (No. 2, July, 1939), pp. 12-13.

14. *The Round Table*, CXXIII (June, 1941).

15. Fred Alexander, *Australia and the United States*, Boston, 1941, p. 55.

16. Hasluck, *The Government and the People*, p. 321.

17. Fred Alexander, "What Americans Think about Australia," *The Austral-Asiatic Bulletin*, IV (No. 5, December-January, 1940-41), pp. 6-7.

18. Alexander, "Australia and the United States," pp. 5-13.

19. Lothian to H. A. McClure-Smith, December 20, 1939, Butler, *Lord Lothian*, p. 271.

20. Gauss to Hull, November 20, 1940, File 711.47/75.

21. Memorandum by Stewart, January 9 and 13, 1941, File 800.01B11 Registration of Australian Information Bureau/2-4.

22. Gauss to Hull, December 1, 1940, File 711.47/74.

23. Gauss to Hull, January 7, 1941, File 711.47/77.

24. File 811.7447, *passim*.

25. Frank R. McNinch, Chairman of the Federal Communications Commission, to Hull, April 22, 1938, File 811.7647/5.

26. Gauss to Hull, January 15, 1941, File 811.7447/35.

27. Gauss to Hull, January 22, 1941, File 711.47/78.

28. Thomas Burke to Berle, Dunn, Atherton, January 9, 1941, File 811.79690 Pan American Airways/377.

29. Gauss to Hull, March 4, 1941, File 711.47/79.

30. Memorandum by Stewart, May 8, 1941, File 711.47/82.

31. Wainwright Abbot, Consul General, Fiji Island, to Hull, August 6, 1942. File 811.79690 Pan American Airways/396.

32. Gauss to Hull, January 15 and 23, 1941, File 811.7447/35-36; Memorandum by Stewart, May 8, 1941, File 711.47/82.

33. Gauss to Hull, January 23, 1941, File 811.7447/36; Memorandum by Francis C. de Wolf, International Communications Division, November 13, 1941, File 811.7447/53.

34. Memorandum by de Wolf, January 30, 1941, File 811.7447/34; Hull to Embassy, London, February 4, 1941, File 811.7447/34; Welles to Embassy, London, July 12, 1941, File 811.7447/41A.

35. Moffat to Hull, telegram, July 7, 1941, File 811.7447/41; Thomas Burke to Assistant Secretary of State Breckinridge Long and Welles, October 27, 1941, File 811.7447/66; Memorandum by de Wolf, November 13, 1941, File 811.7447/53.

36. Hull to Minister Nelson Johnson, telegram, December 13, 1941, File 811.7447/53A.

37. Johnson to Hull, telegram, December 16, 1941, File 811.7447/54; Burke to Ray Atherton and Long, December 24, 1941, File 811.7447/54.

38. *New York Times*, March 13, April 11, June 21 and 25, October 25, 1941, January 18, February 23, June 14, July 3, 1941.

39. New York *Times*, July 5 and September 1, 1941.

40. Moffat to Minter, August 19, 1941, Moffat Papers.

Chapter Ten

1. Grew to Hull, telegram, January 9, 1941, United States, Department of State, *Foreign Relations of the United States: Diplomatic Papers, 1941,* 7 vols., Washington, 1956-1961, V, 8-9.
2. Grew to Hull, telegram, January 12, 1941, *Foreign Relations, 1941,* V, 13-14.
3. Alan Watt, First Secretary of the Australian legation, to Hornbeck, February 1, 1941, *Foreign Relations, 1941,* V, 52.
4. Navy Department to the Department of State, February 4, 1941, *Foreign Relations,* 1941, V, 55.
5. Memorandum by Hornbeck, February 7, 1941, *Foreign Relations,* 1941, V, 60-61.
6. Wigmore, *The Japanese Thrust,* p. 57.
7. British ambassador to the Secretary of State, February 11, 1941, *Foreign Relations, 1941,* V, 74-77.
8. Churchill to Roosevelt, February 16, 1941, *Foreign Relations, 1941,* V, 79-80.
9. Telegram received at the British Embassy from the Foreign Office, February 11, 1941, *Foreign Relations, 1941,* V, 76-77.
10. Memorandum by Hull, February 14, 1941, *Foreign Relations: Japan, 1931-1941,* II, 387.
11. Grew to Hull, February 26, 1941, *Foreign Relations: Japan, 1931-1941,* II, 137-38.
12. Grew to Hull, telegram, February 27, 1941, *Foreign Relations, 1941,* IV, 53-54.
13. Hasluck, *The Government and the People,* pp. 315-23.
14. Memorandum by Hull, February 15, 1941, *Foreign Relations, 1941,* IV, 39-41.
15. Churchill to Roosevelt, February 20, 1941, *Foreign Relations, 1941,* V, 83.
16. Casey to Hornbeck, February 18, 1941, *Foreign Relations, 1941,* V, 81.
17. Memorandum by Hornbeck, March 5, 1941, *Foreign Relations, 1941,* V, 106.
18. London *Times,* March 4, 1941; Alan Chester, *John Curtin,* Sydney, 1943, p. 94.
19. Sydney *Morning Herald,* March 5, 1941.
20. London *Times,* March 6, 1941.
21. Chester, *John Curtin,* p. 95.
22. *Pearl Harbor Attack,* XXXIII, 1196-97; Feis, *Road to Pearl Harbor,* pp. 156-57.
23. Maxwell W. Hamilton to Casey, March 13, File 811.3347/147.
24. Australia, *Commonwealth Parliamentary Debates,* 16th. Parliament, 1st. Session, Volume 166, pp. 118-20.
25. Hull to Johnson, telegram, May 13, 1942, United States Department of State, *Foreign Relations of the United States: Diplomatic*

Papers, 1942, 7 vols., Washington, 1960-, I, 545-46. When lend-lease aid was terminated in 1946 the United States had furnished Australia with £A388,000,000 in goods and services and had received in reverse lend-lease aid from Australia £A261,000,000. Werner Levi, *American-Australian Relations,* Minneapolis, 1947, p. 138.

26. Minter to Hull, March 29, 1941, File 701.9447/12.
27. Doyle to Hull, April 9, 1941, File 811.3347/154.
28. Minter to Hull, March 31, 1941, File 811.3347/146.
29. Doyle to Hull, April 9, 1941, File 811.3347/154.
30. Memorandum by Stewart, May 8, 1941, File 711.47/81.
31. Minter to Hull, March 31, 1941, File 811.3347/146.

Chapter Eleven

1. Robert S. Sherwood, *Roosevelt and Hopkins,* New York, 1948, p. 259.
2. Churchill, *Their Finest Hour,* pp. 435-37.
3. Wigmore, *The Japanese Thrust,* pp. 76, 82-83.
4. *Judgment of the International Military Tribunal for the Far East,* Washington, 1948, pp. 878-82, 923.
5. Hasluck, *The Government and the People,* p. 349.
6. Winant to Hull, telegram, April 19, 1941, *Foreign Relations, 1941,* V, 132.
7. British embassy to the Department of State, April 21, 1941, *Foreign Relations, 1941,* V, 134.
8. Memorandum by Hull, April 22, 1941, *Foreign Relations, 1941,* V, 136-37.
9. Casey to Hull, April 22, 1941, *Foreign Relations, 1941,* V, 137-38.
10. Memorandum by Hull, April 28, 1941, *Foreign Relations, 1941,* V, 139-40.
11. Langer and Gleason, *Undeclared War,* pp. 428-49.
12. Australia, *Commonwealth Parliamentary Debates,* 16th. Parliament, 1st. Session, Vol., 167, pp. 19-20.
13. Feis, *Road to Pearl Harbor,* pp. 197-98; Stimson and Bundy, *On Active Service,* pp. 386-87; Wigmore, *The Japanese Thrust,* p. 81.
14. Kirby, *The War Against Japan,* I, 61-63; Matlof and Snell, *Strategic Planning for Coalition Warfare, 1941-1942,* pp. 65-67.
15. Memorandum by Welles, May 22, 1941, *Foreign Relations, 1941,* IV, 210-12; Memorandum by Hull, May 24, 1941, File 740.0011PW/220; Memorandum by Hull, May 27, 1941, *Foreign Relations, 1941,* IV, 234; Woodward, *British Foreign Policy in the Second World War,* p. 173.
16. Draft proposal handed by Nomura to Hull on May 12, 1941, *Foreign Relations: Japan, 1931-1941,* II, 420-25.
17. Memorandum by Hull, May 9, 1941, File 740.0011EW1939/10949.

18. Minter to Hull, May 24, 1941, File 611.4731/434.

19. *Judgment: IMT*, pp. 926-27.

20. Memorandum by Acting Secretary Sumner Welles, July 24, 1941, *Foreign Relations: Japan, 1931-1941*, II, 527-30.

21. Hasluck, *The Government and the People*, p. 526.

22. Hasluck, *The Government and the People*, p. 526.

23. Feis, *Road to Pearl Harbor*, pp. 242-48.

24. Hasluck, *The Government and the People*, p. 527.

25. Grew to Hull, telegram, August 26, 1941, *Foreign Relations, 1941*, V, 281-82.

26. Feis, *Road to Pearl Harbor*, p. 244.

27. Hasluck, *The Government and the People*, p. 527.

28. Memorandum by Welles, August 2, 1941, *Foreign Relations, 1941*, IV, 359-60.

29. Memorandum by Welles, August 4, 1941, *Foreign Relations, 1941*, V, 254-56.

30. Memorandum by Hull, August 7, 1941, *Foreign Relations, 1941*, IV, 363-64.

31. Memorandum by Hull, August 9, 1941, *Foreign Relations, 1941*, IV, 268-69.

32. Hasluck, *The Government and the People*, p. 529-30.

Chapter Twelve

1. Memorandum by Welles, August 9, 1941, *Foreign Relations, 1941*, I, 345-54.

2. Memoranda by Welles, August 10 and 11, 1941, *Foreign Relations, 1941*, I, 354-63; Winston S. Churchill, *The Grand Alliance*, Boston, 1950, pp. 439-40; Woodward, *British Foreign Policy in the Second World War*, pp. 175-76.

3. Hasluck, *The Government and the People*, p. 531.

4. Churchill, *Grand Alliance*, p. 448.

5. Oral statement handed by Roosevelt to Nomura, August 17, 1941, *Foreign Relations: Japan, 1931-1941*, II, 556-57.

6. Hasluck, *The Government and the People*, p. 534.

7. *Foreign Relations: Japan, 1931-1941*, II, 549-770, *passim*. In September, 1941, E. Stanley Jones, a missionary who had long resided in the Far East, proposed to the Department of State that Japan be offered New Guinea as compensation for the evacuation of China. He reported to Department officials that he had taken the proposal up with Casey and had found the Australian minister sympathetic. The Department of State and the White House evidenced little enthusiasm for the scheme, and it is likely that Canberra's reaction was the same. *Foreign Relations, 1941*, IV, 455-57, 501-02, 555-58, 561-62, 613-16, 641, 702-03.

8. Quoted in Feis, *Road to Pearl Harbor*, p. 264.

9. *Pearl Harbor Attack*, XX, 4022-23. The formulation of the text

of this decision and its various translations are analyzed in Butow, *Tojo and the Coming of the War,* pp. 246-59.

10. Grew to Hull, telegram, August 19, 1941, *Foreign Relations, 1941,* IV, 382-83; Memorandum by Hornbeck, August 21, 1941, *Foreign Relations, 1941,* IV, 384-87; Grew to Hull, telegram, August 30, 1941, *Foreign Relations, 1941,* IV, 416-18; Memorandum by Hornbeck, September 5, 1941, *Foreign Relations, 1941,* IV, 425-28; Grew to Roosevelt, telegram, September 22, 1941, *Foreign Relations, 1941,* IV, 468-69; Memorandum by Joseph W. Ballantine, September 23, 1941, *Foreign Relations, 1941,* IV, 470-75; Grew to Hull, telegram, September 29, 1941, *Foreign Relations, 1941,* IV, 483-89; Memorandum by Hornbeck, October 2, 1941, *Foreign Relations, 1941,* IV, 493-94.

11. Feis, *Road to Pearl Harbor,* pp. 282-84; *Judgment: IMT,* pp. 950-53. Butow states that though some naval leaders opposed war, the Navy general staff agreed with the Army general staff that war should be undertaken. Butow, *Tojo and the Coming of the War,* pp. 262-84. In mid-October the Naval General Staff made the final decision to incorporate into the overall offensive plans the plan for the attack on Pearl Harbor. Louis Morton, *The War in the Pacific: Strategy and Command, the first Two Years (United States Army in World War II),* Washington, 1962, pp. 105-07.

12. Whitington, *The House Will Divide,* pp. 68-73; Hasluck, *The Government and the People,* pp. 491-505.

13. Langer and Gleason, *Undeclared War,* pp. 742-50.

14. Australia, *Commonwealth Parliamentary Debates,* 16th. Parliament, 1st. Session, Vol. 168, p. 303.

15. Whitington, *The House Will Divide,* pp. 56-61, 74-95; C. Hartley Grattan, "Australia's New Labour Government," *Current History,* I (1941-1942), 333-39.

16. Whitington, *The House Will Divide,* p. 97.

17. Stimson and Bundy, *On Active Service,* p. 388.

18. The reinforcement of the Philippines is discussed fully in Louis Morton, *The War in the Pacific: The Fall of the Philippines* (United States Army in World War II), Washington, 1953, ch. iii.

19. Watson, *Chief of Staff,* pp. 424-43; War Department to Commanding General, United States Army Forces in Far East, September 30, 1941, and War Department to Special Army Observer, London, September 30, 1941, *Foreign Relations, 1941,* IV, 497-99.

20. Hull to Winant, telegram, October 15, 1941, and Hull to Johnson, telegram, October 15, 1941, *Foreign Relations, 1941,* I, 573-75.

21. Hasluck, *The Government and the People,* pp. 537-38.

22. Memorandum by Hamilton, October 8, 1941, File 811.24546/8; Wesley Frank Craven and James Lea Cate, editors, *The Army Air Forces in World War II: Plans and Early Operations, January 1939 to August 1942,* Chicago, 1948, pp. 178-93.

23. Hasluck, *The Government and the People,* p. 538.

24. Johnson to Hull, telegram, October 18, 1941, *Foreign Relations, 1941,* I, 575-76.

25. Hasluck, *The Government and the People,* p. 538.

26. Hull to Johnson, telegram, October 23, 1941, *Foreign Relations, 1941,* I, 578; Hull to Johnson, telegram, October 24, 1941, File 811.24546/18.

27. Memorandum by Stewart, October 22, 1941, File 811.24546/17.

28. Diplomatic contact between the United States and Australia had also been extended with the appointment of American military and naval attachés to Canberra in August. The appointment of these officers without prior consultation with Australia caused embarrassment in Canberra. The Japanese government had been urging the exchange of military and naval attachés and the Australian government, not wishing to admit such Japanese attachés, had insisted that the exchange of attachés was a question of mutual agreement and reciprocity and by no means followed automatically from the establishment of diplomatic relations. When the Australian government informed the Department of State of its embarrassment, it was agreed that the exchange would take place on a basis of agreement and reciprocity, though Australia might defer the appointment of attachés to Washington. Memorandum by Stewart, August 15, 1941, File 121.5447/4.

29. Churchill, *Grand Alliance,* pp. 588-90; Hasluck, *The Government and the People,* p. 543.

30. Churchill, *Grand Alliance,* pp. 591-92.

31. Churchill, *Grand Alliance,* pp. 592-93.

32. Langer and Gleason, *Undeclared War,* pp. 843-47.

33. *Pearl Harbor Attack,* XIV, 1061-67.

34. Hasluck, *The Government and the People,* pp. 547-48.

35. Page, *Truant Surgeon,* p. 314.

Chapter Thirteen

1. Document handed by Nomura to Hull, Nov. 7, 1941, *Foreign Relations: Japan, 1931-1941,* II, 709-10.

2. *Pearl Harbor Attack,* XI, 5420; Feis, *Road to Pearl Harbor,* pp. 302-03; Current, *Secretary Stimson,* p. 154.

3. Churchill, *Grand Alliance,* p. 594.

4. *Pearl Harbor Attack,* XIX, 3683-85.

5. *Pearl Harbor Attack,* XII, 155-56.

6. Draft proposal handed by Nomura to Hull, November 20, 1941, *Foreign Relations: Japan, 1931-1941,* II, 755-56. The drafting of these terms is discussed in Butow, *Tojo and the Coming of the War,* pp. 314-26.

7. *Pearl Harbor Attack,* XII, 100, 165.

8. Memorandum by Hull, November 22, 1941, *Foreign Relations, 1941,* IV, 640. The text of the American draft is given in *Foreign*

Relations, 1941, IV, 635-40. See also Woodward, *British Foreign Policy in the Second World War,* pp. 179-80.

9. *Pearl Harbor Attack,* XIV, 1124-31; *Foreign Relations, 1941,* IV, 642-46.

10. Memorandum by Hull, November 24, 1941, *Foreign Relations, 1941,* IV, 646-47; Woodward, *British Foreign Policy in the Second World War,* pp. 181-82.

11. Hasluck, *The Government and the People,* pp. 549-50.

12. Hasluck, *The Government and the People,* pp. 549-50.

13. Hasluck, *The Government and the People,* p. 550.

14. *Pearl Harbor Attack,* XIV, 1162-66; Memorandum by Hull, November 25, 1941, *Foreign Relations, 1941,* IV, 654-55; British embassy to the Department of State, November 25, 1941, *Foreign Relations, 1941,* IV, 655-56; Woodward, *British Foreign Policy in the Second World War,* pp. 181-83.

15. *Pearl Harbor Attack,* XIV, 1300; Churchill, *Grand Alliance,* pp. 596-97; *Foreign Relations, 1941,* IV, 665.

16. Text is given in *Foreign Relations: Japan, 1931-1941,* II, 764-70.

17. *Pearl Harbor Attack,* XI, 5422; Current, *Secretary Stimson,* p. 158.

18. Memorandum by Hull, November 27, 1941, *Foreign Relations, 1941,* IV, 668.

19. Hasluck, *The Government and the People,* p. 550.

20. Memorandum by Hull, November 29, 1941, File 711.94/2561.

21. Hasluck, *The Government and the People,* pp. 550, 553.

22. Halifax reported to London that Hull "ought not to have acted in this way." Woodward, *British Foreign Policy in the Second World War,* p. 184.

23. Hasluck, *The Government and the People,* pp. 552-53.

24. Kirby, *The War Against Japan,* I, 173-74.

25. Hasluck, *The Government and the People,* pp. 553-54.

26. Hasluck, *The Government and the People,* p. 554.

27. Page, *Truant Surgeon,* p. 318.

28. Woodward, *British Foreign Policy in the Second World War,* pp. 186-87.

29. Hasluck, *The Government and the People,* pp. 555-56; Wigmore, *The Japanese Thrust,* p. 109; Wood, *The New Zealand People at War,* pp. 205-06. On the day after Australia learned of the American assurance, the United States Naval attaché at Singapore, John M. Creighton, cabled Admiral Thomas C. Hart, Commander of the Asiatic Fleet at Manila, reporting that Brooke-Popham had received a message from London telling of the assurance of armed support. When Creighton was questioned in the congressional investigation of the Pearl Harbor attack, he testified that he was reporting only a rumor. The congressional investigators were unable to uncover further evidence regarding the matter. See *Pearl Harbor Attack,* II, 491-96, 502-04, 508; X, 4802-09, 4818-19, 5080-89; XI, 5514-16.

30. Kirby, *The War Against Japan,* I, 177-86; Wigmore, *The Japanese Thrust,* pp. 121-25.

31. Stimson and Bundy, *On Active Service,* p. 390.

32. Further clarification of Roosevelt's commitment may be possible when the full text of Halifax's dispatches from Washington are opened to historians, but unless the British government modifies its fifty-year rule, those records will not be available until the year 1991. It is unlikely that records of the Roosevelt-Halifax conversations will ever be found on the American side, for it was Roosevelt's conscious policy not to record conversations. Further discussion of the question is found in Raymond A. Esthus, "President Roosevelt's Commitment to Britain to Intervene in a Pacific War," *Mississippi Valley Historical Review,* L (June, 1963), pp. 28-38.

33. *Pearl Harbor Attack,* XI, 5165-66.

34. Japan's decision for war is discussed in Butow, *Tojo and the Coming of the War,* pp. 343-63.

Chapter Fourteen

1. Dunn to Moffat, October 1, 1936, Moffat Papers.

2. See John Biggs-Davison, *The Uncertain Ally,* London, 1959, *passim,* and the study by an American scholar, Leon D. Epstein, *Britain—Uneasy Ally,* Chicago, 1954, pp. 57-77.

3. Lord Halifax, *Fullness of Days,* New York, 1957, pp. 256-58.

4. Memorandum by Welles, August 9, 1941, *Foreign Relations, 1941,* I, 345-54.

5. Memorandum by Welles, August 4, 1941, *Foreign Relations, 1941,* V, 254-56.

6. Halifax, *Fullness of Days,* pp. 250-54.

7. Halifax, *Fullness of Days,* p. 270. A similar assessment is given on p. 296.

8. Hasluck, *The Government and the People,* p. 527.

Bibliography

UNPUBLISHED SOURCES

Note: Australia, like the United Kingdom, follows the fifty-year rule, and therefore Australian records on external affairs in the 1930's will not be open to the historian until the 1980's. The principal sources on the American side are the Department of State records and the Moffat papers. These sources complement one another, for the Moffat papers contain few official records but many letters written by the principal Department of State officials concerned with Australian affairs. The Hull papers contain little other than duplications of Department records.

Records of the Department of State, National Archives and Department of State, Washington, D.C.

Files:

033.4711	740.0011EW1939
124.47	740.0011PW
611.4731	747.94
641.031	800.01B11 Registration of Australian Information Bureau
647.003	811.24546
647.006	811.3347
647.116	811.71247H
647.9431	811.7447
700.0011 Pacific	811.7647
701.4711	811.79690 Pan American Airways
701.4794	841.248
701.9447	847.00
711.415 Traders	847.01B11
711.47	847.248
711.472	847.415
711.94	893.154

Papers of Cordell Hull, Library of Congress, Washington, D.C.

Papers of Jay Pierrepont Moffat, Houghton Library, Harvard University, Cambridge, Massachusetts.

PUBLISHED SOURCES

United States Government Documents

Note: The *Foreign Relations* series gives an extensive selection of documents on United States-Australian relations in the 1930's. The volumes dealing with the diplomacy preceding the outbreak of the Pacific war are excellent and give virtually the complete record from Department files.

United States, Bureau of Foreign and Domestic Commerce (Department of Commerce). *Trade of the United States with Australia . . . 1938-.* Washington, 1938-.

United States, Congress. *Pearl Harbor Attack: Hearing of the Joint Committee on the Investigation of the Pearl Harbor Attack.* 39 vols. Washington, 1945-1946.

United States, Department of State. *Papers Relating to the Foreign Relations of the United States: Japan, 1931-1941.* 2 vols. Washington, 1943.

———. *Papers Relating to the Foreign Relations of the United States, 1927.* 3 vols. Washington, 1942. Vol. I.

———. *Papers Relating to the Foreign Relations of the United States, 1931.* 3 vols. Washington, 1946. Vol. I.

———. *Foreign Relations of the United States: Diplomatic Papers, 1934.* 5 vols. Washington, 1950-1952. Vol. I.

———. *Foreign Relations of the United States: Diplomatic Papers, 1935.* 4 vols. Washington, 1952-1953. Vol. II.

———. *Foreign Relations of the United States: Diplomatic Papers, 1936.* 5 vols. Washington, 1953-1954. Vol. I.

———. *Foreign Relations of the United States: Diplomatic Papers, 1937.* 5 vols. Washington, 1954. Vol. II.

———. *Foreign Relations of the United States: Diplomatic Papers, 1938.* 5 vols. Washington, 1954-1956. Vol. II.

———. *Foreign Relations of the United States: Diplomatic Papers, 1939.* 5 vols. Washington, 1955-1957. Vol. II.

———. *Foreign Relations of the United States: Diplomatic Papers, 1940.* 5 vols. Washington, 1955-1961. Vols. I, III, IV.

———. *Foreign Relations of the United States: Diplomatic Papers, 1941.* 7 vols. Washington, 1956-. Vols. I, III, IV, V.

United States, Tariff Commission. *An Analysis of the Trade Between Australia and the United States.* Prepared in response to Senate Resolution 334, 72nd Congress, 2nd Session, February, 1934.

Australian Government Documents

Note: The *Parliamentary Debates* is the only important source among the Australian published documents. The Department for External Affairs' *Current Notes* does not recount Australian diplomacy but merely gives general information on world affairs.

Australia, Parliament. *Commonwealth Parliamentary Debates.*

———. *Commonwealth Parliamentary Papers.*

Australia, Department for External Affairs. *Report, 1936.* Canberra, 1936.

———. *Report, 1937.* Canberra, 1937.
———. *Current Notes on International Affairs.* Fortnightly, Canberra, 1936-.
Australia, Eastern Mission. *The Australian Eastern Mission, 1934* (Report of the Right Hon. J. G. Latham, Leader of the Mission). Canberra, 1934.

Memoirs and Diaries

Note: The Australian memoirs by Hughes and Pearce contain little on United States-Australian relations. The memoirs of Page are more useful for the present study, but even this voluminous account has relatively little on American affairs. Churchill's works give extensive coverage of both Anglo-Australian relations and Anglo-American relations. Eden's account seldom mentions Australia. Halifax gives an excellent general discussion of his activities in the United States. Hull's memoirs reveal little that is not found in the Department records.

Blum, John Morton. *From the Morgenthau Diaries.* Boston, 1959.
Churchill, Sir Winston S. *The Gathering Storm.* New York, 1948.
———. *The Grand Alliance.* Boston, 1950.
———. *Their Finest Hour.* Boston, 1949.
Eden, Anthony. *The Memoirs of Anthony Eden, Earl of Avon: Facing the Dictators.* Boston, 1962.
Grew, Joseph C. *Ten Years in Japan.* New York, 1944.
———. *Turbulent Era.* 2 vols. Boston, 1952.
Halifax, Lord. *Fullness of Days.* New York, 1957.
Hooker, Nancy Harvison, editor. *The Moffat Papers: Selections from the Diplomatic Journals of Jay Pierrepont Moffat, 1919-1943.* Cambridge, Massachusetts, 1956.
Hughes, William Morris. *Crusts and Crusades: Tales of Bygone Days.* Sydney, 1947.
———. *Policies and Potentates.* Sydney, 1950.
Hull, Cordell. *The Memoirs of Cordell Hull.* 2 vols. New York, 1948.
Ickes, Harold L. *The Secret Diary of Harold L. Ickes.* 3 vols. New York, 1953-1954.
Page, Sir Earle. *Truant Surgeon: The Inside Story of Forty Years of Australian Political Life.* Sydney, 1963.
Pearce, Sir George Foster. *Carpenter to Cabinet: Thirty Seven Years of Parliament.* London, 1951.
Stimson, Henry L., and McGeorge Bundy. *On Active Service.* New York, 1947.

Biographies

Note: On the British side the biographies of Lothian and Chamberlain are most useful. Australian biographies are not numerous, and those that exist contribute little to the present study. On the American side the biographies of Stimson are valuable sources on the coming of the Pacific war.

Butler, J. R. M. *Lord Lothian (Philip Kerr), 1882-1940.* London, 1960.
Chester, Alan. *John Curtin.* Sydney, 1943.
Churchill, Randolph Spencer. *The Rise and Fall of Sir Anthony Eden.* London, 1959.
Current, Richard N. *Secretary Stimson: A Study in Statecraft.* New Brunswick, 1954.
Feiling, Keith. *The Life of Neville Chamberlain.* London, 1946.
Morison, Elting E. *Turmoil and Tradition: A Study of the Life and Times of Henry L. Stimson.* Boston, 1960.
Whyte, W. F. *William Morris Hughes: His Life and Times.* Sydney, 1957.

The United States and the Pacific

Note: The studies by Butow, Feis, and Langer and Gleason are the only first-rate, comprehensive accounts of the coming of the Pacific war. Among the official histories, those by Matlof and Snell and by Watson are most valuable on matters of grand strategy.

Butow, Robert J. C. *Tojo and the Coming of the War.* Princeton, 1961.
Craven, Wesley Frank, and James Lea Cate, editors. *The Army Air Forces in World War II: Plans and Early Operations, January 1939 to August 1942.* Chicago, 1948.
Feis, Herbert. *The Road to Pearl Harbor: The Coming of the War Between the United States and Japan.* Princeton, 1950.
Ferrell, Robert H. *American Diplomacy in the Great Depression: Hoover-Stimson Foreign Policy, 1929-1933.* New Haven, 1957.
Grattan, C. Hartley. *The United States and the Southwest Pacific.* Cambridge, Massachusetts, 1961.
Griswold, A. Whitney. *The Far Eastern Policy of the United States.* New York, 1938.
International Military Tribunal for the Far East. *Judgment.* Washington, 1948.
Langer, William L., and S. Everett Gleason. *The Challenge to Isolation, 1937-1940.* New York, 1952.
———. *The Undeclared War, 1940-1941.* New York, 1953.
Levi, Werner. *American-Australian Relations.* Minneapolis, 1947.
Matlof, Maurice, and Edwin M. Snell. *Strategic Planning for Coalition Warfare, 1941-1942 (United States Army in World War II).* Washington, 1953.
Morison, Samuel Eliot. *History of United States Naval Operations in World War II: The Rising Sun in the Pacific.* Boston, 1948.
Morton, Louis. *The War in the Pacific: The Fall of the Philippines (United States Army in World War II).* Washington, 1953.
———. *The War in the Pacific: Strategy and Command, the First Two Years (United States Army in World War II).* Washington, 1962.

Schroeder, Paul W. *The Axis Alliance and Japanese-American Relations, 1941*. Ithaca, 1958.

Sherwood, Robert E. *Roosevelt and Hopkins*. New York, 1948.

Smith, Sara R. *The Manchurian Crisis, 1931-1932: A Tragedy in International Relations*. New York, 1948.

Watson, Mark S. *Chief of Staff: Prewar Plans and Preparations (United States Army in World War II)*. Washington, 1950.

Wohlstetter, Roberta. *Pearl Harbor: Warning and Decision*. Stanford, 1962.

Australian External Affairs

Note: The British, Australian, and New Zealand official histories of the Second World War are the most valuable sources in this category. These works, based upon records still closed to historians, contain detailed accounts of British and Australian diplomacy. Long quotations or paraphrases of key documents are included. The volume by Woodward is the most important source on British diplomacy, though the studies by Butler and Kirby are also valuable. Among the Australian studies, the volume by Hasluck is the most valuable source on diplomacy. Wigmore's study gives an excellent account of the military-strategic aspect of the story. The New Zealand history by Wood is a good source on the Pacific policies of Australia and New Zealand.

Alexander, Fred. *Australia and the United States*. Boston, 1941.

Australian Institute of International Affairs. *Australia and the Pacific*. Princeton, 1944.

——. *Australia and the Pacific* (Australian Supplementary Papers: British Commonwealth Relations Conference, 1938). Lapstone, 1938.

——. *Australian Policies, Political and Strategic* (Australian Supplementary Papers: British Commonwealth Relations Conference, 1938). Lapstone, 1938.

Ball, William Macmahon, editor. *Press, Radio and World Affairs, Australia's Outlook*. Melbourne, 1938.

Bassett, R. *Democracy and Foreign Policy: A Case History, The Sino-Japanese Dispute, 1931-1933*. London, 1952.

Butler, J. R. M. *Grand Strategy: Volume II, September 1939-June 1941 (History of the Second World War)*. London, 1957.

Carter, Gwendolen. *The British Commonwealth and International Security: The Role of the Dominions 1919-1939*. Toronto, 1947.

Casey, Richard Gardiner. *Friends and Neighbours: Australia and the World*. Melbourne, 1954.

Cutlack, Frederic Morley. *The Manchurian Arena: An Australian View of the Far Eastern Conflict*. Sydney, 1934.

Duncan, Walter George Keith, editor. *Australia's Foreign Policy*. Sydney, 1938.

Grattan, C. Hartley, editor. *Australia*. Berkeley, 1947.

————. *Introducing Australia.* New York, 1947.

Hancock, W. K. *Australia.* Sydney, 1945.

Harris, Harold L. *Australia's National Interests and National Policy.* Melbourne, 1938.

Hasluck, Paul. *The Government and the People, 1939-1941 (Australia in the War of 1939-45).* Canberra, 1952.

Horsfall, J. C. *Australia.* New York, 1955.

Hughes, William Morris. *Australia and War To-day: The Price of Peace.* Sydney, 1935.

Kirby, Major General S. Woodburn. *The War Against Japan (History of the Second World War).* 3 vols. to date. London, 1957-.

Mansergh, Nicholas. *Survey of British Commonwealth Affairs: Problems of External Policy, 1931-1939.* London, 1952.

McGuire, Frances Margaret. *The Royal Australian Navy, Its Origins, Development and Organization.* Melbourne, 1948.

Price, Archibald Grenfell. *Australia Comes of Age: A Study of Growth to Nationhood and of External Relations.* Melbourne, 1945.

Ross, Ian Clunies, editor. *Australia and the Far East: Diplomatic and Trade Relations.* Sydney, 1935.

Shepherd, Jack. *Australia's Interests and Policies in the Far East.* New York, 1940.

Whitington, Don. *The House Will Divide: A Review of Australian Federal Politics in the Past Twenty-Five Years.* Melbourne, 1954.

Wigmore, Lionel. *The Japanese Thrust (Australia in the War of 1939-45).* Canberra, 1957.

Wood, F. L. W. *The New Zealand People at War: Political and External Affairs (Official History of New Zealand in the Second World War, 1939-45).* Wellington, 1958.

Woodward, Sir Llewellyn. *British Foreign Policy in the Second World War (History of the Second World War).* London, 1962.

Australian Economics and Trade

Note: Though Australians have produced many good works on economics and trade, the studies include little on United States-Australian trade relations. In addition to the books here listed, many volumes of documents dealing with finance and trade during 1929-1937 have been published.

Allin, Cephas Daniel. *Australian Preferential Tariffs and Imperial Free Trade.* Minneapolis, 1929.

Australian Institute of International Affairs. *Australian Economic Policies* (Australian Supplementary Papers: British Commonwealth Relations Conference, 1938). Lapstone, 1938.

Brigden, J. B., D. B. Copland, C. H. Wickens, E. C. Dyason, and L. F. Giblin. *The Australian Tariff: An Economic Enquiry.* Melbourne, 1929.

Cleary, V. F. *British Imperial Preference in Relation to Australia.* Washington, 1934.

Copland, Douglas B. *Australia in the World Crisis, 1929-1933.* New York, 1934.

Copland, Douglas B., and C. V. Janes, editors. *Australian Trade Policy: A Book of Documents, 1932-1937.* Sydney, 1937.

Duncan, Walter George Keith, editor. *National Economic Planning.* Sydney, 1934.

Garnett, Arthur C. *Freedom and Planning in Australia.* Madison, 1949.

Hancock, W. K. *Survey of British Commonwealth Affairs: Volume II, Problems of Economic Policy, 1918-1936.* London, 1940.

Hitchins, F. Eric. *Tangled Skeins: A Historic Survey of Australian Wool Marketing.* Melbourne, 1956.

MacLaurin, William R. *Economic Planning in Australia, 1929-1936.* London, 1937.

Nicholson, D. F. *Australia's Trade Relations: An Outline History of Australia's Overseas Trading Arrangements.* Melbourne, 1955.

Shann, Edward Owen Giblin. *An Economic History of Australia.* Melbourne, 1948.

Walker, Edward Ronald. *Australia in the World Depression.* London, 1933.

Windett, Nancy. *Australia as Producer and Trader, 1920-1932.* London, 1933.

Wood, Gordon Leslie. *Australia: Its Resources and Development.* New York, 1947.

Articles

Note: The periodical literature on Australian external affairs in the 1930's is made up almost entirely of accounts by contemporary observers.

Alexander, Fred. "Australia and the United States," *The Australian Quarterly*, XIII (1941), 5-13.

―――. "What Americans Think About Australia," *The Austral-Asiatic Bulletin*, IV (1940-1941), 6-7.

"American and Australia's Defense," *The Austral-Asiatic Bulletin*, III (1939-1940), 14-15.

"Australian Policy in the Pacific," *The Austral-Asiatic Bulletin*, IV (1940-1941), 5.

Casey, Richard G. "Australia in World Affairs," *Australian National Review*, II (1937), 2-12.

Dennett, Tyler. "Australia's Defence Problem," *Foreign Affairs*, XVIII (1939), 116-26.

Esthus, Raymond A. "President Roosevelt's Commitment to Britain to Intervene in a Pacific War," *The Mississippi Valley Historical Review*, L (1963-1964), 28-38.

174 · *Bibliography*

Friedman, Irving S. "Australia and Japan: Conflict in the South Pacific," *Political Science Quarterly*, LII (1937), 392-406.

Grattan, C. Hartley. "An Australian-American Axis?" *Harper's Magazine*, CLXXX (1939-1940), 561-69.

———. "Australia and Japan," *Asia*, XXXVIII (1938), 689-92.

———. "Australia and the Pacific Stalemate," *Asia*, XLI (1941), 169-71.

———. "Australia through Australian Eyes," *Asia*, XLI (1941), 613-17.

———. "Australian Self-reliance," *Asia*, XL (1940), 11-14.

———. "Australia's New Labour Government," *Current History*, I (1941-1942), 333-39.

Hall, Basil. "Australia and the Pacific," *National Review*, CV (1935), 600-06.

Lawrence, O. L., and G. H. Palmer. "The Economic Consequences of Ottawa in the Pacific Dominions," *Documents of the Fifth Conference of the Institute of Pacific Relations*, Banff, Alberta, 1933.

Morgan, Arthur C. "Sino-Japanese Sidelights," *Australian National Review*, II (1937), 8-13.

Index

Abbott, Edwin, 53
Air bases, 120-21
Alexander, Fred, 90-92
Amalgamated Wireless, 94, 96
American Telephone and Telegraph, 94
Atherton, Ray, 33
Atlantic Conference, 114-16, 121
Australia: ties with England, 3, 4-6; navy, 4, 63; trade, 4, 6-8, chs. ii, iv, v, 110, 135-37, 143n; diplomatic contact with U.S., 5-6, 30-31, 67-69, 71, 89, 154n, 162n; Matson shipping dispute, 9-10, 28-30, 34-35; Manchurian crisis, 10-11; relations with Japan, 10-11, 19, 21-23, 34, chs. vii-xiii *passim;* Parliament, 18-19, 41, 42, 52, 118-19; Pacific Pact proposal, 32-33; visits of U.S. warships, 50-51, 82-83, 102-04, 107; Austrian Anschluss, 62-63; Anglo-Italian negotiations, 63-64; Czechoslovakian crisis, 64-66; change of ministries, 67, 118-19, 119-20; rapprochement with U.S., 69, 90-92; wartime import licensing, 71-72; question of U.S. armed support in Pacific, 75, 80, 111, 112-13, 114-16, 121, 131-34, 139-40; Singapore staff conferences, 83-84, 108; economic sanctions, 84-85, 111-12; Washington staff conference, 86; publicity activities in U.S., 92-93, 96-97; radio-telegraph communications, 94, 96; Pan American Airways, 94-96; war scare, 100; Lend-Lease, 102-03, 159-60n; defense against Japan, 105-06; Atlantic Conference, 114-16; U.S. air bases, 120-21; U.S. diplomatic leadership in the Pacific, 123-24, 131-32; *modus vivendi* proposal, 126-30
Austria, 62, 63

Beaseley, J. A., 101
Benes, Eduard, 65

Berle, Adolph A., Jr., 72-73, 79, 80
Bingham, Robert W., 25, 33, 38
British Commonwealth and Empire, 75-76, 110-12, 114, 116, 123, 125, 136, 137-38. *See also* Great Britain.
Brooke-Popham, Sir Robert, 131, 133, 164n
Brown, Gordon, 47
Bruce, Stanley Melbourne, 13, 25, 65, 68, 113, 132
Burma Road, 73, 75-76, 79, 80, 81

Cadogan, Sir Alexander, 139
Caldwell, John K., 13
Cameron, Archie, 18
Cameron, Sir Donald, 19
Canada, 40, 53, 54, 57, 65, 68, 96
Canberra government: *see* Australia
Casey, Richard G.: trade diversion, 21, 39-40; Anglo-American relations, 25; U.S.-U.K. trade treaty, 38; defense expenditures, 63; becomes Minister of Supply and Development, 67; appointed Minister to the United States, 71, 154n; requests U.S. declaration of war, 72; status quo of N.E.I., 72-73; possible Far Eastern settlement, 73-74; aid to French Indochina, 78-79; Burma Road, 79, 80; possible U.S. armed support in the Pacific, 80, 113, 140; proposes U.S. naval visit to Australia, 82-83; proposes U.S. naval visit to Singapore, 82, 83, 88; Singapore staff talks, 84; economic sanctions, 84-85; publicity activities in U.S., 92, 93, 95, 96-97; war scare, 100; warnings to Japan, 106-07, 110, 112, 134; Japanese-American conversations, 109; *modus vivendi* proposal, 126, 127, 128, 130; New Guinea, 161n
Chalkley, Harry O., 10, 25
Chamberlain, Neville, 23-24, 37, 63-66, 70
Chiang Kai-shek, 122, 129

175